B$10⁰⁰

FATHER'S FOOTSTEPS

DAMON RUNYON, JR.

Father's Footsteps

RANDOM HOUSE   NEW YORK

For

Patricia,
D'Ann *and* Damon III

FATHER'S FOOTSTEPS

1

Ours was a house divided by a dark secret.

My father and I were at odds for many years. Separated by distance, we did not communicate with each other for months at a time. There was a void of silence between us. He was dying of cancer when the chance came to bridge this gulf.

By then he was voiceless. His larynx had been removed because of the cancer. His talking was reduced to scrawlings on pads—terse comments on this and that. He tired easily.

My father discovered quite by accident that he had cancer. He had taken a dog to an animal hospital. While there the veterinarian became suspicious of my father's throat. The vet urged him to see a specialist immediately.

In short order a battery of the best medical brains in the country were shaking their heads over him. The consensus was that his larynx had to be removed immediately to save his life. The disease had been discovered much too late.

Actually he was worse off than anyone knew then. It wasn't the larynx alone that was invaded—the trachea, or windpipe, also was affected. So that had to come out, too, with a metal tube inserted as a substitute. The pipe stuck out of his throat and had to be covered with gauze bibs. Cells of the original growth already were on their way to other parts of the body and, as is the usual course, struck the nearest lymph glands on the left side of the neck. These were removed in a second operation and it was after that, in September, 1944, that I visited him in New York Memorial Hospital. I was allowed five minutes to work out the puzzles of two lifetimes.

He was drowsy with drugs and in pain, too weak for much talk. I jabbered about going to Cincinnati that night on a new job with Radio Station WSAI. I had to stretch for an optimistic pitch. This might be the last time we would see each other. There was so much to say—yet again the silence fell between us. The time was hardly enough for more than the exchange of cordial inanities. How could the vast empty spaces of two lifetimes be bridged within minutes with Death standing by?

Finally I reached out and took my father's hand. It was probably the first time I had held his hand since I was a little boy learning to walk. I stood there silently holding his hand. Time waited. The bridge was begun.

As soon as I arrived in Cincinnati I started the first steady correspondence with my father which, after one break of eight months, lasted until his

death, and provided his only intimate thoughts put
to paper.

My dear Son:
Thanks for your nice letter. I was glad to see you
even though it was only for a minute. I feel better
now and am able to be about a bit but still am heavily
bandaged. The greatest handicap of this whole business is, of course, the loss of voice, but what the hell!
I guess I have said too much in time as it is. . . .
I know Cincinnati very well, or rather I should
say I used to know it, as I imagine there have been
many changes since I was there last. It is one of my
favorite towns. . . .
You are right about radio. It is very interesting
and exciting. I think you make no mistake learning
that game. I believe the day of high salaries in the
newspaper business is over and just beginning in
radio. Your audience is so much greater there is no
comparison.
Watch your health. That is about the only advice
I have to give nowadays. No one takes advice anyway.
Write me again if you get the opportunity.
Affectionately,
Dad

My father was a product of the six-gun West. At
one time somewhere in his prowls as a youth he
actually packed a six-gun. He still had such a weapon
when I was very small, but it was just another dust-
catcher around the apartment in New York City.

His father was an Indian fighter with red hair and goatee, and a temper to match. He later was a tramp newspaperman wandering from place to place and leaving little for history to record. His name was Alfred.

He married Elizabeth Damon. Between them they gave my father his full name, Alfred Damon Runyon. They had two daughters. That's about all I ever knew of them—my father almost never talked of family. He had what amounted to a phobia against close relationships, particularly family.

His mother died shortly after his birth in Manhattan, Kansas, where his father was working at the moment. Who raised the children I don't know—they may have been farmed out to kind neighbors, as was the custom. Grandpa Runyon later showed with his boy in tow around Pueblo, Colorado.

My father was left to his own devices as a small boy. His father, no family man, liked to debate with the town mouths at the bar. My father was a lonely, barefoot little boy about town.

This background molded the man Runyon, as well as the writer. The loss of a mother, and the lack of a real father at so early an age, made him wary of forming close relationships for fear of losing them. The man grew up silent since there never was anyone in whom to confide his inner thoughts.

Grandpa Runyon started his boy in the newspaper profession as a printer's devil, an ink-stained wretch of the composing room, who swept floors and fed lead to the hellbox. The boy Runyon also worked as a bellhop learning the inner whisperings of the hotel trade and once tried his whip hand as a horse jockey.

In these growing days he acquired a veneer of hardness covering a heart of loneliness.

He was a reporter already dabbling with words when he heard the call of the Spanish-American War. Legend put him down as fourteen and it long was officially believed he was the youngest soldier in that war. As is usual with legends, the facts are not so colorful. He was eighteen. He looked fourteen and had difficulty enlisting because recruiting officers couldn't believe it. He always took advantage of this young look and let it be believed he was four years younger than he was. My father loved the Army. His favorite tune was the bugle blast "To the Colors." He went to the Philippines and came back in two years without a scratch from musket or mosquito. The most dangerous shots he encountered were those that came at him over a bar.

At an early age my father became what he called a rumpot, or what is termed today an alcoholic. Not until late in life did he tell me his story, and then only because I had fallen into the same pit.

The first week of October, 1944, after seeing my father in the hospital, I went to Cincinnati as news editor of Radio Station WSAI, with prospects of going on the air as a commentator. The future sparkled bright, but I lasted just five weeks. I got potted—and fired.

For I was a drunk and had been from the age of nineteen when I fell to earnest drinking while a Washington correspondent. In seven years I had gone the route of the rummy—d.t.'s and the sanitariums at twenty-three, jails, job losses, the psycho ward of the city hospital, and finally Alcoholics

Anonymous. For eight months my father heard no word from me.

He conducted no espionage, for the Runyons followed the live-and-let-live formula and this wasn't the first long silence. At last I wrote him a report explaining that I had hit the gutter gone in booze but had reached an island of safety by falling into the hands of Alcoholics Anonymous. I told him I didn't know what his reactions would be to virtual public admission of my plight, but that I was convinced it was my only hope for tomorrow and I was going to stick to it regardless of what he thought.

I added that I didn't know how much truth there was to the report that he, too, had had to fight the booze. In all his advice to me as a boy he had dropped only slight hints. They were included in other advice which I studiously ignored, because he was inclined to hand down opinions without embellishment: "Don't drink and don't marry."

I might have seen some sense in the first part if there had been any in the second. As it was, I ignored both. My report from Cincinnati brought a quick reply from my father with the story of his own battle with the bottle.

July 3, 1945

My dear Son:

I was delighted to hear from you and greatly relieved as I did not know just where you were or what you were doing.

To say that I am pleased with your good report is putting it very mildly. It is the best news I have heard in a long time.

I think the samples of your work that you sent me are excellent reporting with a swell human interest touch. I have always thought you could write and it has always been my hope that you would carry on what I think is an honorable name in the newspaper game, the greatest profession in the world.

You will improve the more you write. Good writing is simply a matter of application but I learned many years ago that the words will not put themselves down on paper in dreams or in conversations.

You have been on my mind a great deal lately. Mary [1] and I were having dinner at Lindy's one night recently and I wrote her a note (my only means of communication with people now) saying I wondered where you were.

"I have been thinking of him all day," she said. "It's his birthday."

She was as pleased as I was with your letter. . . .

I know more about Alcoholics Anonymous than you might think. I read a great deal about the organization and I had several personal contacts with active participants on the Pacific Coast. One worked at Fox when I was making *Irish Eyes Are Smiling.*

I think it may be one of the great movements of all time and I am extremely pleased that it has aroused your interest.

Surely by this time you must have learned that you were not cut out for a drinking man. Drinking is not hereditary as some rumpots like to alibi, but I think there are certain strains that are allergic to alcohol and you seem to carry that strain.

[1] My elder sister, who at that time was staying temporarily with our father in his suite at the Buckingham Hotel.

You ask me about my own experiences. I quit drinking thirty-five years ago in Denver and have not had a drink since. I quit because I realized that I got no fun out of drinking. Liquor only gave me delusions of grandeur that got me into trouble. It never made me happy and bright and sparkling as it does some people. It made me dull and stupid and quarrelsome. It made me dreadfully ill afterwards. I did not have the constitution to drink. It rendered me helpless. It destroyed my pride, my sense of decency.

I quit because I saw that I was not going to get anywhere in the world if I didn't, and I wanted to go places. I was sorely tempted many times, usually in moments of elation over some small triumph or when I was feeling sorry for myself, a strong characteristic of the drinker, but I managed to stand it off.

It was never taking that first drink that saved me.

I had to endure loneliness and even derision as a result of my abstinence for some years but it eventually became a matter of such general knowledge that no one pressed me to take a drink any more and finally I became positively famous for hanging out with drunks and never touching a drop.

We could have saved many a great career with an organization like the A.A.'s in the old days when a lush was shunned even more than he is today.

You stick to your organization and try to help other fellows unfortunate enough to be under the spell of old John Barleycorn. No good ever comes of drinking and I don't think any bad ever comes of *not* drinking.

So much for my temperance lecture, except that I have only a little time left as you may surmise from my ailment, but I will go happy if I know that you have conquered your enemy. If you have gone eight months without drinking, you would be a fool to ever start again, knowing what you know.

I will be sixty-five in October. I get around all right and feel pretty well but I live under a shadow. I have to see the doctor every week. I do my daily column and a Sunday feature and last month I wrote two fiction stories for *Collier's*.

I have to keep plugging away at an age when I thought I would be in retirement, because my illness practically broke me. I went to Hollywood at a salary of over $2,000 a week largely as a matter of satisfying my vanity—I thought it was wonderful to be able to command that kind of income at sixty-three —forgetting that it only added to my normal income and increased my taxes.

Well, the upshot was the government taxes took most of it, and when I became ill and the big money was shut off entirely the doctors and the hospitals cut up what was left. I am now living not only on borrowed time but practically on borrowed money. But having seen others similarly afflicted I know that I have no kick coming.

Your A.A.'s should give you something you never had—sympathy for your fellow man. It was not your fault that you didn't have it. It was just the way you were gaited.

That is one element a writer must have to be a good writer—sympathy. What we call "heart" . . .

I will not again write you at this length. But I am so glad to hear that you are getting along all right I am a little windier than usual.

I am quite pleased that we are in opposing papers. I have been in the *Enquirer* off and on for years—usually off. You are with a fine outfit, the Scripps-Howard. I think it is better for a young writer than any other. The kind of work you are doing is exactly the kind you need because it gives you human contacts and a knowledge of how people live.

You say that you don't know if you will ever be anything more than a better than average reporter. Well, my boy, I think that is better than being king. I do indeed.

Mary sends her love and I sign myself in deepest affection.

Dad

At one fell swoop a bridge crashed across the gulf that had separated my father and me for so many years. Alcoholics can establish between themselves relationships based on mutual understanding even at levels where words fail.

All accounts agree that my father was a two-fisted shot lifter beginning back in San Francisco after the Spanish-American thing. He migrated to Denver, then the queen city of the West and a rip-snorting newspaper town where a circulation war was on full blast under the Bonfils-Tammen reign.

My father worked variously for the Denver *Rocky Mountain News,* now a Scripps-Howard paper, the *Denver Post,* and some other sheets now deceased and forgotten.

On the *News* my father was smitten by a smart-stepping young girl named Ellen Egan, a society reporter and a good one according to the recollection of her associates. She was what he would call a handsome woman with a personality that sparkled with love of life.

My father was a diamond in the rough. My mother was a lady. She liked diamonds—polished. She saw the potential value of this one and evidently toyed with the idea of working a reformation. Her friends and co-workers advised against.

They were right, of course. A woman's a fool to try to reform a rumpot, as many have found after years of trying. Ellen Egan was advised to wait until he had his fill of booze. Apparently the stand-off routine worked.

"Al" Runyon, as he then was known, wanted to go places and Ellen Egan represented the places he wanted to go. Her father was a railroad superintendent, a high and mighty position in those days when the snorting iron horse represented power in the fast sprouting West. If he didn't rate society he was just a cut beneath.

Her mother was one generation removed from Ireland. Mary Morris Egan was a five-foot gentle woman whose hair was white as the caps of the Rockies when she was a girl. Her honeymoon was at a junction high in the mountains where she was set at once to preparing bear steaks for the crew bosses throwing a railroad over the shoulders of the West.

The rugged life of the West then was interwoven with the new citified ways of the nation. The rough weave of mountain cloth was wed in the foothills to the lace of the drawing room. The Egans who wrestled with railroad ties in the clouds struggled with silk ties in Denver below.

They had a chesty house on a so-called good street, a sprawling box of many rooms set on a broad lawn where you could hit a baseball without breaking a window. Those were the days when you could exhale without cooling your neighbor's soup.

In summer nights the neighbors sat under bold shade trees big enough to defy the sky. The elders rocked and fanned and rocked and fanned while the younger set played croquet, with maybe a little side game of coquet. When darkness moved in they took to the drawing room for a big evening of singing around the family piano.

Past this lawn line of inspection Al Runyon used to troop in high-button shoes, tight-top trousers and a straw boater sitting jack deuce on his head, a string anchoring the hat to his collar so sly breezes wouldn't launch it down the street. The lawn rockers bobbed faster and the fans whirred and word would go down the line: "Tsk-tsk, there goes that Alfred Runyon calling on the Egan girl."

If *that* Alfred Runyon heard he never let on. His eye was on a star.

As my father and I continued our long distance get-together by mail in 1945, we clashed when my sister suddenly vanished as she was inclined to do since suffering in 1944 what was popularly called "a nervous breakdown."

In alerting me in the event she should show up in Cincinnati, he snapped that I should notify him instantly as I probably would be unable to handle the problem. This attitude irked me since he had ignored her plight when it first had become obvious, and had left everything to me, but now was playing the boss.

In replying I pointed out he was being unnecessarily distrustful. I observed that if I'd received such a letter before joining A.A. I might have wound up throwing myself on the mercy of Demon Rum. My sister eventually did show up in Cincinnati shortly afterward and I had her hospitalized—in fact, I took all responsibility except for finances.

Dear Damon:

. . . I am of course delighted to learn that you are still on the wagon but with your reference to your ominous suggestion as to what might have been the consequences of that letter, let me say that a sobriety subject to reactions of the nature you mention under any circumstances is not on a very solid foundation.

I have remained sober for thirty-five years now after having been a far worse alcoholic than you can possibly conceive and I leave it to your own imagination as to the emotional shocks I must have had in that period—distress and sorrow and everything else.

I never took any bows for being sober. It was selfish on my part. I wanted to be successful and I had to put booze out of my life to achieve that end. I never felt that I was doing anyone a favor by staying sober except myself. . . .

I am glad to learn of your progress generally. Keep up the good work. If you will give me a home address I will send you a batch of shirts that you may be able to use as I am no longer able to wear garments of that particular type.

Bestest
Dad

While Ellen Egan refused to marry Al Runyon, or Alfred as she always called him, until he fought Demon Rum to a decision, that was not the reason he quit. That may have nudged him a little, but the alcoholic can quit only for himself.

He quit for himself because he wanted to be successful, and that was the driving motive behind him the rest of his years. Success. What was success? Mainly a beautiful wardrobe and woman to match.

The barefoot boy wanted handmade shoes. The motherless lad sought love of a woman on a pedestal. The fatherless child kept floundering in pitfalls.

A girlhood friend of my mother's reported they came upon Al Runyon trying to thrash the dust from his clothes in front of the *Denver Post* building. The way she put it, he'd just been tossed out of the city room. A binge had left him with battered face from some bout at the bar.

He felt so badly about being seen in such condition he didn't want to walk down the street with the girls. My mother wasn't one to let that bother her. They got on a horsecar together, but then my father wouldn't sit with her.

Of such events is the cure for alcoholism concocted. There is none other. The alcoholic suffers unspeakably, but neither fancy clothes nor beautiful women can make him stop. No matter how much the horrors come in the night, the victim of booze can be saved only by himself, and then only if he's convinced he's worth saving. By believing in Al Runyon it's possible that Ellen Egan played the second role.

At any rate he quit the swinging door routine and they were duly married with the ceremony, but not the pomp, of the Roman Catholic church. They had to be wed in the rectory since my father wasn't a Catholic. The Denver society columns carried long accounts which barely mentioned the groom: "Ellen Egan Marries Denver Poet."

At that time my father fancied his talent lay in poetry and he ground out a good deal of verse published by such outlets as *The Denver News* and the *Denver Post, New York Sun, The Denver Times,* the *Army and Navy Journal, People's Magazine, Leslie's, Lippincott's Magazine, Munsey's Magazine, Spare Moments* and the *Bohemian Magazine.*

His poetry like that of many other aspiring young writers of the day sounds now like a poor man's Kipling. Much of it was about soldiering in the Spanish-American War and the Philippines or about other sports of less deadly nature.

In his sportswriting days he was inclined to poetic prose, at least in the leads, as were most other sportswriters. He must have thought well of his own efforts for he would recite at the drop of a hint, which I would drop, feeling it would please him, and he would stand at attention while delivering the militaristic lines of such verses as his own "To the Colors":

"It isn't on th' firin' line you feel th' battle thrill,
    An' it isn' dodgin' bullets wot you know are
      meant to kill;
An' it isn't when the bandmen play some patri-
    otic air
That you feel th' fever in yer blood an' wanter
    rip an' tear—
But let th' ole familiar break come in th' tune
    they play;
A silence for a moment an' you hear th' captain
    say:
'Port Arm.' an' then th' air is split as though by
    shrapnel shell—
'To th' Colors.' sing th' bugles an' it's then you
    wanter yell."

One verse achieved fame in sports-reading circles
years later, in 1924, when jockey Earle Sande was
injured in a horse fall at Saratoga. He declared he'd
never ride again. Such items were treated as catas-
trophes in those sports-crazy days and my father
pulled out the stops:

"Maybe there'll be another,
    Heady an' game, an' true—
Maybe they'll find his brother
    At drivin' them horses through.
Maybe—but, say, I doubt it.
    Never his like again—
Never a handy
Guy like Sande
    Bootin' them babies in."

Besides giving printers fantods from setting such
apostrophe-riddled type my father apparently also

gave himself a boot with that one for he liked it well enough to play on it fourteen years later when Sande won the Kentucky Derby in 1940:

> "Say, have they turned the pages
>   Back to the past once more?
> Back to the racin' ages
>   An' a Derby out of the yore?
> Say, don't tell me I'm daffy,
>   Ain't that the same ol' grin?
> Why it's that handy
> Guy named Sande,
> Bootin' a winner in."

My father had two books of poetry published, *Tents Of Trouble* and *Rhymes Of The Firing Line*, but he put aside the poet's mantle professionally except for lapses like the Sande lead and occasions when he would drop into a baseball story something like this:

> "Count that day lost when slow descending sun
> Hears no umpire called one son-of-a-gun."

There was no money in poetry. He wanted to be a success. And wasn't money the American standard of success? So he spent most of his time and efforts getting the money. He did not stop to consider whether there might be something wrong with the standard of measurement.

After Ellen Egan and Alfred Runyon were married they went east to the big city, where my father had landed a job on the *New York American*. The fact that he could get a first-rate post was evidence of his ability, because he was taken despite an impressive drinking record. Editors were tolerant of boozers partly because the best newspapermen in those days were fast men with shot glasses.

My father already was a top feature writer in Denver when he came to New York in 1910. William Randolph Hearst, who owned the *American*, among other papers, paid his lead men well and my father earned the princely sum of $65 a week.

New York was the goal of newspapermen then and represented a certain amount of success. My mother and father took instantly to the city and never again looked west with any particular longing, and she made only a few trips home. They became New Yorkers although early circumstances forced them to live in rooming houses in Flushing, Long Island.

The Golden Era of Sports, or Age of Wonderful Nonsense, was just beginning. My father's flair for feature stories made him sure fire for the sports department. He started to travel on sports stories. In 1912, for example, he roamed with the New York Giants with colleagues like Heywood Broun. Of course no one had any inkling of the heights they would scale. Broun didn't even get a by-line in those days.

From sports my father was detached for special duty on such reportorial-writing assignments as Black Jack Pershing's pursuit of the bandit Pancho Villa in Mexico. When the United States entered World War I he went to France with the U. S. First Army. Every assignment carried him toward the stars—and away from home.

My father held he was keeping his end of the marriage deal if he won all the bread a breadwinner could win. The rest was left to the wife. Raising children, managing a home, and such workaday chores were out of his province and he viewed them with the detached air of an innocent bystander, except perhaps to render decision in some case calling for high court judgment, such as whether to buy one of those newfangled radios.

His view of women was that of the wild West period of America. All women, whether from society or the streets, were greeted with grave courtliness, an imperceptible bow beginning in the lumbar region, an elaborate sweep of the hat as if fanning the air, and a low (to denote respectful) "How do you do?"

"Be respectful to your sister!" my father raged at me even when I was just at the hair-pulling stage. "Don't ever talk back to your mother!" I don't think he got accustomed to night clubbing in later days with women in the party, especially if they were ladies of the family and the stage show happened to be unclean or undressy. The woman's place was in the home, although it was getting more difficult to keep her there.

I never heard my father use the slightest swear word in front of women and he disapproved loudly of double-meaning jokes in mixed company. The same went for children, of course, and I was a Washington correspondent in my twenties when I first heard him use backroom words in the company of men. It startled me—I didn't know he could swear.

All his copy was clean. He never used a word or suggestive idea in print that couldn't be spoken with ladies present. This was true even in his short stories of guys and dolls when he was dealing with what were known in polite company of the jazz era as gold diggers. Back where he came from the cavalier treatment was extended down to the blowsy woman of the town swilling wretched whiskey in a frontier honky-tonk. "Remember, boys, she may be somebody's mother."

Women belonged to another world that was changing so fast that it was bewildering to his kind. A woman was a dear and priceless luxury, to be handled with care, an ornament for the arm, a treasure to show off to the boys. Any ideas or comments she might have, say, on the state of the union, were to be taken lightly, like a musical comedy or an airy opera where the contralto trilled unintelligible nonsense.

"Women," he once sighed to me behind the door. "You can't live with 'em, and you can't live without 'em. They're nice to have around, especially if they're not bad-looking, if they don't get any big ideas. Sometimes I just like to listen to 'em prattle along, you know, the way they do when they're not really saying anything. I just like to listen to their voices and look at 'em. But sometimes," his face clouded, "I wish they'd go jump in the river. This, of course, is just between you and me."

2

My sister was born August 24, 1914 at home.
Mother, always dramatic, cried, "If I'm going to die
in childbirth I'll do it at home! No hospital for me!
Besides, imagine being born in a hospital!" My sister, named Mary Elaine, was premature and an in-
cubator had to be improvised. She weighed two
pounds. My father was busy edifying the public
about a more world-shaking event, a baseball game.
He was similarly occupied when I uttered my first
protest, also at home, June 17, 1918.

By then my father was writing a column and
spent considerable space that day on his own version
of "Little Red Riding Hood." Under a heading "By
A. Mugg" he explained he'd been reading the tale
to his daughter at home and considered the story
worth passing along. The column was done in essentially the same style he used years later to write
about guys and dolls.

The odds were against my sister from the start.

When she was four months old she weighed only eight pounds, which was my weight at birth. While doctors aren't convinced, it would appear obvious that a child born too soon would be more susceptible to psychological or physical ills unless extra attention was given. As the first child she naturally got plenty of cooing in the beginning when father was closer to home and the ménage was not so regimented toward fame and fortune.

Under the heading "First Steps" in the baby book mother kept on Mary, there was recorded in mother's fine rounded hand: "December 1915, The little Weela [1] could by crawling and holding to the wall visit her daddy's room and knock at his door." (Such a disturbance would be rewarded in later years by whacks.) "January 1916 . . . The baby walked across the room unaided. . . ." "First corsage bouquet, November 19, 1916. Her father took her riding in a hansom and bought her a corsage bouquet of one pink rose, one spray lilies of the valley, and fern, in a regular holder. First hansom cab ride." Mary then was two.

Mother also noted "The Songs We Sang" as "Hello, Frisco, Hello," "I Love You Truly, Truly Dear" and "My Little Girl." In writing her from ventures afar father also addressed mother as "My Little Girl." One of the two times I ever saw him cry was when "My Little Girl" was played on the radio while we were in Miami about a year after her death.

---

[1] There is no explanation of what "Weela" means, whether it is just one of those noises made by doting parents and adopted as a nickname or whether it might be an Indian name. I incline to the former definition.

We children had perambulators that were in the Cadillac class as carriages go but this ostentation was more front than real evidence of wealth. They usually were parent-powered, but sometimes either maids or friends were put to horse. In 1950 Gene Fowler wrote me this recollection:

"You might be amazed to know that I sometimes wheeled you in a baby buggy over toward the river. Of course some prankster might say, why in hell didn't we both go into the river?

"However, I was assisting your wonderful mother and was accompanied by my then only child, Gene Jr., who was in the same buggy. It was a bit crowded to be sure, but we all got the air that day.

"I don't suppose you remember the times when you afterward played on the roof of our apartment on Amsterdam Avenue with the kids of our neighborhood.

"You can see from the foregoing that senility is setting in and I am becoming garrulous and foolishly reminiscent. At the time of which I speak our families were indeed closely associated. I was about the age that you now enjoy." [about thirty-two]

In the days recalled by Fowler—who became the highest paid screenwriter in Hollywood—he and my father were struggling young newspapermen who eagerly looked forward, of necessity, to each pay check. They went each day to the office to labor for Hearst.

Fowler, Runyon, Arthur "Bugs" Baer and cartoonist TAD (T. A. Dorgan) ranked as humorists on the old *New York American* under the stern-faced editorship of Arthur Brisbane, who was noted among the staff for his lack of a sense of humor.

However, Brisbane fully appreciated the need for chuckles in the daily paper. He got around his own blind spot for humor by seeking out one of his humorists whenever a story or picture puzzled him.

"Look at this," he'd say. "Is it funny?"

On one score there would have been no doubt in his mind. Brisbane had an oversized head and an equally large argument purporting to prove that a big dome was a sign of superior intelligence. However, he never found out that behind office doors his nickname—invented by my father—was "Double Dome."

My father's sense of humor more often than not completely escaped me because of his fierce appearance. He had the habit of going around with a long face, conveying the impression that inside, too, he was a sourpuss.

"Around the office," an old-timer recalled, "he appeared very moody, as if he was all burning up inside. But then when he would stop and talk he would be very courteous and pleasant. And he and Baer, TAD and Fowler were always pulling some stunt."

My father looked the same around home and as a child I thought he was angry with me. I was forever trying to figure out what I might have done to displease him. I feared to talk to him in these moods so I didn't find out he actually was "very courteous and pleasant." It wasn't until later that I learned he was a prankster.

In his office days the old *American* was a gay place to work, before the newspaper became serious big business, and by all accounts my father enjoyed himself there. However, he was inclined to get stern and deliver dead-pan lectures, in the high twang his voice took on when he got caustic, to try to make heavy drinking colleagues reform.

There was happiness in our home then. My father was going places with hard work, and he had a smart-looking young woman to take with him. Ironically, the higher they stepped together the more they lost that original glow of the cozy home.

Dear Damon:

I sent you a batch of stuff that you may or may not be able to use. Anything you can't use yourself, pass on to some friend. As you will perhaps surmise, it is all expensive truck and some of it could not be duplicated today.

In this connection, I have been weeding out my wardrobe and I have several old suits and overcoats that I was going to distribute locally when the thought occurred to me that in your A.A. work you may occasionally have to outfit some bloke and perhaps you can make use of these garments. They would be too big for you unless you have picked up a lot of heft since the last time I saw you.

I was about your build and weight at your age and did not pick up weight until after I had my appendix and tonsils out. Now I weigh nearly 190 pounds, which of course is much too much. I am considered a great knife-and-fork man and suppose I should go on a diet, but why? Where am I going?

. . . [The statue] [2] is a big heavy thing, a poig-

---

[2] The statue mentioned in this letter was a two-and-a-half foot high bust of a handsome girl incongruously wearing a

nant reminder of all the Runyon households from 111th Street to Bronxville—112th, 116th, 94th and Broadway, etc., etc. I imagine you have a memory of some of them. Our first home was on 111th where Mary was born; then we moved to 112th or maybe it was 113th where you were born.

We lived a long time on the top floor of 116th and Riverside Drive where I had the penthouse on the roof to work in.

I think perhaps I liked best the home on the top floor of the old apartment building at 94th and Broadway looking down on the corner of 95th, then one of the haunts of the bootleggers and gangsters of the period.

It was a lively place to live and easy of access and it was there you had turtles and canaries and other live creatures. The last place we lived before your mother moved to Bronxville was at 113th and the Drive, a somewhat elaborate apartment that I never liked. I have only unpleasant memories of it.

In affection,
Dad

All the Runyon homes he mentioned still stand and I've gone back to see if they'd evoke any particular emotion. They don't. The first Runyon home I re-

---

tricorner Napoleonic hat. We always called it "the Napoleon." Made of porcelain, with delicate beadlike trimmings, it had been a sentimental gift from my father to mother in the days when there still was sweetness between them. It had stood in all our homes.

It was all that was left of those days and somehow Mary had managed to hold onto it, lugging it around even in her erratic travels, without breaking it. How or why she did this remained a mystery to my father and me.

membered was the building at 251 West 95th Street on the corner of Broadway. My father was mistaken in his report on the location. We had the apartment on the top, or seventh floor, overlooking Broadway and 95th Street. The lively corner was at 96th Street and Broadway. He also was mistaken about the location of our last Riverside Drive home. It was at 102nd, not 113th Street.

The first memory I have of any kind is related to the place at 95th Street and Broadway. I remember committing a nuisance, then running to a corner and facing out for defense against attack from the rear. Obviously my mother had been at batting practice with a hairbrush, her major offensive weapon. I reckon I then was about three.

My father of those years is remembered only as a vague presence—I am unable to call up any actual picture of him. Yet there were events involving him which I well remember. There was the case of the blood on the window sill below.

My father used to go hunting with a bunch of the boys come duck season near Havre de Grace, Maryland. Once he hung a string of duck corpses out the window of the 95th Street apartment when my mother banned them from the icebox. A neighbor below yelled blue bloody murder. Blood from the deceased had dripped down and was absorbed by an expensive coat she had put out for an airing on her window sill.

My mother told my father in no uncertain terms that thereafter she would take care of the food department by going to stores like civilized people did —never mind the big hunter act.

One memory of my father does come back from those days to haunt—the ghost of a promise made to a small boy. My father continued his yearly trips to Maryland to sit in the bogs with the boys in hopes of outsmarting some weary birds. With bugging eyes I used to sit in on the preparations, the oiling of shotguns, the counting of shells, the saddle soaping of boots, the packing of hunting jackets with their many strange pockets.

For my benefit there was much target practice— without ammunition, of course. My father would fix an imaginary duck in the sights of his shotgun and follow it across the ceiling. Suddenly "Pow! Pow!" I could see the feathers fly every which way and the duck in a limp dive toward the cold water as the hunting dogs went flopping into action. Each year my father made me a promise.

"Next year," he said, "I'll take you with me. Yes, sir! Next year without fail we'll go hunting together and Pow! Pow!" I always looked forward to going on that trip with my father, but he never took me. He always promised—and forgot. Many years later at his funeral, carrying the urn with his ashes, I remembered that promise and thought, "Well, at last we're going on that trip together."

My father brought home all the live creatures we had around the house. I remembered a batch of tadpoles mainly because when they came of age they vanished from the tank one by one. We never found any of them and that always puzzled me.

Then there was Rastus, a cockroach. He was my father's friend.

One year—I was about four judging from snapshots—our mother took my sister and me to Pasadena, California. Why or for how long I don't recall. All I remembered were the roses that stabbed me with their thorns, the kids who persuaded me to sit on a lawn spray which I'd never seen before, Gyp the Airedale who saved me from being run over—and Rastus.

My father wrote my mother long, lively letters explaining his improved method of keeping house. Example: Never make beds—they only get mussed up again. He cooked for himself, probably the only time he was unable to complain about how breakfast was done.

He told my mother not to worry about him getting lonely because he had a newly acquired friend. He discovered—it was an unexpected shock the first time—that Rastus slept at night in his bedroom slipper. Thereafter he was careful to rouse Rastus first in the morning. His friend didn't eat enough to miss and was company to have around the house.

When my mother returned home Rastus had to go. She discovered he'd brought a lot of his pals in with him. She thought he must be no account to take advantage of a friendship like that. She thought some of my father's other friends were not much better.

He fell to gabbing with the corner sharps in jazzbo getups who stood around making gimlet eyes in front of a corner cigar store. These bootleggers, thugs and gangsters provided my father with the characters and knowledge that were to go into fiction yarns that probably established him in literary history and eventually made him the highest-priced short story writer.

Later it came to be believed that "Damon Runyon characters" were inspired by the Broadway set around Lindy's and that they all spoke in the present tense style in which he told his short stories. Actually the Lindy's circle provided inspiration for later characters, but the real originals were from uptown Broadway. As for the present tense, my father had been using that for years before he ever got into the downtown Broadway whirl.

One of the characters on our corner once sidled up to my father when he'd become known around and about. This rogue's gallery model, his hands in pockets to make sure no pals checked his funds, looked about cautiously and then whispered hoarsely to my father, "If you ever miss anything upstairs leave me know. I will see that you get it back."

This kind of thing made my mother nervous and made my father famous. In a summing up he recalled to what heights he'd soared on the strength of such low characters.

Dear Damon:

. . . I am going back into Memorial Hospital about Saturday or Sunday for an operation designed to permit me to dispense with the tube in my trachea which would be an enormous relief. [He didn't.]

I am unable to do any talking as yet and doubt that I ever will. I was sixty-five years old on October 3 and am somewhat surprised that I have gotten this far, so all the time I get from here in is velvet.

I have an offer from *Cosmopolitan* magazine of $5,000 per story for twelve stories per year which strikes me as a trifle ironical as it comes at a time when I could not possibly muster the physical energy for even a third that much work, while in the period of my greatest activity, when I might have been able to do it, they paid no attention to me.

Your Alcoholics Anonymous seems to be doing a fine work here in New York. It is coming to be accepted as a standard organization. . . .

I wish I might have continued to live in Beverly Hills and stayed in the movies. I enjoyed the life out there and enjoyed making pictures. My *Big Street* finally showed a profit and my *Irish Eyes* made over a million (for the studio). Sixteen of my short stories were made into movies which may be some kind of a record.

. . . Take care of yourself and write me again soon.

In affection.
Dad

My father's progress as a writer could be measured by the homes where we lived. Each was better than the last and there was no slipping back.

The apartment at 95th Street and Broadway was a sort of halfway point, so he was to recall later that was the one "I liked best." The man at the top of success has to worry about staying there, so he may not be much happier than the fellow looking up with starry eye from the bottom.

My father usually was off to the chores, covering the routine sports extravaganzas of the day or on detached duty to enlighten the *American's* readers on the spectacles of patriots brawling and braying in convention or on the public display of some moron collared for wife-hacking.

My mother bustled about their coterie of friends, for in that more leisurely day it was possible to maintain such luxuries. Most of these acquaintances had come originally from Denver and clung together like lost children in the big city, but some my mother came to know in the front yards of New York.

Mother always insisted on living hard by some park "for the children" and this was one of the demands that increased the push for success since rents in New York go up according to the number of trees nearby.

However, my sister and I were kept indoors most of the time because mother feared the bandits and other creatures of prey whom she believed infested the city, and she also apparently was hoping the automobile was only a fancy that would pass away with time.

We were so hard put for something to do we spent much time in a game called "I See Something." This was played sitting in the seventh floor window overlooking Broadway. Bars kept us from toppling out the windows, a child hazard common to New York City. Each would name colors of an object and the other was to try and guess what it was. The checkered taxis of the day weren't fair because they were too easy—black and yellow.

A summer amusement for the family—less the father—was to perch on the roof where we could see down a block to the roof garden theatre of the Japanese Garden, a movie house which adjourned showings to the open air when weather permitted. This was called air conditioning. The movies were silent so we didn't need to be any closer. However, we always had the guilty feeling that we were cheating.

I said "less the father" because he was becoming more conspicuous by his absence away at work.

Family and friends saw him less and less. Little groups of intimates drifted apart as each moved higher—and away. In later years this loss to the big city and the demands of success came back to my father to assault him with doubts.

My dear Son:

I will . . . endeavor to get off a stack of clothes to you that I have been piling up. If the stuff sent from Florida fitted maybe some of this will, too, especially an Abercrombie coat I had built for myself years ago which I always thought was one of the smartest garments I ever owned. If not, it will come in handy in your A.A. work . . .

Now then with reference to your remarks about Cincinnati. If I had it all to do over again, knowing what I know now, I would live my life in a town about that size—not too large, not too small, where human companionships are possible, and a man can make friends.

Strange as it may seem, for all my long residence in New York City, I could not have made the swift contacts and produced the influences that you did out there . . . and which seem to have been the result of friendships.

Don't sell that kind of place short. And if you

eventually settle down to doing what I tell you, writing stories (and about Cincinnati perhaps) the town will make no difference one way or the other. . . .

In Affection,
Dad

The Runyon family's move to 320 West 102nd Street on Riverside Drive meant we had arrived. Back then, when an auto going thirty miles an hour was speeding, Riverside Drive was the Gold Coast of New York. The view overlooking the Hudson River was considered worth doubling the rent.

Riverside Park then was a mass of greenery and even wooded in spots. Ash dumps and open railroad tracks, where freight engines spit cinders into the air, scarred the area at water's edge. In summer slum urchins, bald bare, used the Hudson as a swimming hole, diving from ash heaps into rank filth. Nevertheless the area was considered attractive from a distance.

We moved into a seven-room apartment which the tabloids would label lavish and baggage-smashers heaved in with a lot of new furniture and a Steinway grand piano. What brought all this on was my father's rise to the rank of sports columnist. Hearst was paying his sportswriting stars the first fabulous salaries in the newspaper profession. My father signed a contract calling for $25,000 a year, which was money in those days.

My father introduced me into the newspaper profession when I was didy-high to a city room spittoon. There was no prior consultation with me as far as I can remember. It just was assumed without saying that the son should follow in the father's footsteps.

The first step in the process was to take me to the *New York American* office, a sinister-looking rookery busy with the noisy confusion attending the printing of a big city newspaper. At night, when my father would be muttering over his typewriter, the place was frightening to a child of five.

The building was at William and Duane streets, a short stagger off the Bowery where the racket of the Third Avenue elevated overpowered the noises of derelicts brawling, the clattering of horsecarts, the snorting and grinding of autos, and the printers and other press men who were milling about the business of rushing the news to the public.

The *American* was one of the few newspapers of the day that wasn't on Park Row a block away. The area had been infested with saloons to catch the paper trade until Prohibition. When the speakeasy came in vogue there was no noticeable diminution of the sloppy staggering of the Bowery bums or the more distinguished teetering of the fourth estate.

Ancients on the *American,* now the *New York Journal-American,* remembered my father's chauffeur bringing me to the office to wait for him. Actually there was more than one chauffeur, all hired by my father for my mother's convenience. She regarded them as gangsters and treated them as such. There was a heavy turnover in the job. As far as I know only one was what could be termed a gangster. They all were "heavy types," the idea being that they could serve as bodyguards by scaring with their looks, but they seemed amiable gorillas. They probably were unemployed heavyweights.

The wastepaper basket was an unheard of affectation in a newspaper office and I most well remember the paper and other debris that nearly reached my knees. A drunken reporter could fall there and never be found. Over all was the deafening uproar of bells ringing, editors bawling, presses roaring.

To keep me off my father while he labored, the cartoonists drew pictures or I was given a pastepot, pencils and paper to amuse myself. One day my father announced it was time I pitched into the racket. He gave me his copy and directed me to give it to the sports editor. I got lost in the jungle of paper, cuspidors and braying editors and would be there yet if I hadn't been rescued.

This first failure as a copy boy was only one of many that made my father sigh with disappointment over me as a son and wonder if it were worth the time and trouble to attempt to thrust me into the ranks of the ink-stained. I think he persisted only because he felt it was the tiresome duty of a father.

The evidence shows that I was an unexpected surprise to my parents. They kept a complete record on my sister four years earlier, even to her first word, but of my early days the only notice was some formal studio portraits at pablum stage.

However, most writers like my father seem to feel duty-bound by a mysterious law to have a son who will carry on the name, so my father pressed on with the chore of training me. Even when I was a gawking youth not yet at razor age, almost everyone I met demanded a statement on whether I was following in father's footsteps. I never could figure out why anyone would care.

At an early age I'd grown weary of the question, mainly because I couldn't think of a suitable answer besides a blunt "no." I tried a few attempts at humor, all of them weak, such as that I was trying to keep from falling into his footsteps, but eventually I fell back on mumbling, which everyone seemed to accept as a suitable reply.

While my father trained me in certain realms of writing he never actually gave me any aid in getting a job or selling any of my labors until at the last, when I mentioned a motion picture idea a friend of mine and I had in mind. I sought advice on whether an agent or some other mysterious power was required to break into the Hollywood scene.

Dear Son:

Thanks for your letter. I have been under the weather slightly and am staying indoors . . .

About your scenario-writing efforts. If your partner in crime has been in Hollywood he probably knows the ropes himself, but if you like you can send the finished product to me and I will give it to an agent out there with my blessing, which might be the best way. . . . I think an agent gets better results unless one is on the ground and can make direct contacts.

I had several letters from Henry B. Henson after he got out of the Army and went out of my way to try to help him because of his kindness to you and believe I was of some service to him. I did not know of his untimely end and am sorry to hear of it. He seemed to me a man of considerable class. It is odd that I missed the item about him.

I am glad to learn of the progress that your branch of the A.A. is making.

I think this is by far the most important of all these movements and the one that seems likely to become permanent.

I hear considerable of it around New York, and I expect one day to see it a part of state government everywhere.

I am delighted that your interest in it continues to the point of enthusiasm. Naturally you will encounter resistance and disappointment in spots but that happens to everyone in every field of human endeavor. . . .

In affection
Dad

Henry B. Henson was United Press bureau manager at Cleveland when I went to work there and he taught me the actual process of news gathering and writing. My father's training was more general and he was inclined to favor fiction writing in his lectures.

As a pedagogue my father was highly entertaining, perhaps too much so. His method was to spin yarns that set my jaws agape when I was very small. His stories were full of clang and clash, just what a little boy would order. The drawback to this method of teaching was that I didn't believe him. I thought he was telling a lot of stretchers to be amusing.

A wealth of his adventures went in one ear and out the other because I felt they were a little highflown to be true. He was telling the truth, of course, even if he did overreach in spots. As I grew older I came to realize this and bent a more attentive ear.

Class began after he woke up at noon. His rising was a part of the ritual in the strict regime into which our home life settled by the time we had arrived, on Riverside Drive. Since he worked on a morning newspaper he lived mostly late hours and the household had to be grimly quiet until stirrings were heard from his room.

He spent an hour emitting groans and other agonized noises and trying to sneak back to oblivion. He was impossible to deal with during this hassle with himself and the children were warned away. Finally he would face the new day and fling open his bedroom door announcing to whom it might concern, "I'm up." The communiqué would filter down to us through channels. "Your father is up." Then we could go whooping in.

He was subjected to the usual amount of child trivia reporting events of the household which had transpired while he slept: "Ernie's sick." [our canary bird] "Mommie got up early today." "I hurt myself." He pursued these subjects while he shaved, with us watching wide-eyed at the wondrous faces he made, or he delivered brief lectures injected with bits of caustic humor, if he felt good, or philosophy, if he didn't.

We had to leave while he bathed and then he would pad out in slippers and robe to breakfast. This meal had to go perfectly or a storm would break. The eggs had to be done exactly three and one-half minutes, the bacon and toast just so, and he could judge instantly if anything had gone amiss. He ate alone at a big dining room table where he could read all the newspapers.

He went through every newspaper, muttering, grumbling and grousing at the state of affairs. Occasionally he would be struck by some new imbecility of the human race and this would fetch a loud "Hah!" All the time he was stoking up with loud relish.

To a small child he presented the appearances of a fierce fellow. This illusion was heightened by the constant storm warnings from the women folk, "Don't bother your father." I can remember waiting at the dining room door to be noticed by chance when he might glance up from his papers during the fruit and before the egg.

If he did he would absent-mindedly grunt recognition like an Indian chief and I could trot in and request a performance of "the egg trick." By this I meant the hocus-pocus whereby he could make the hen's effort, sitting in the small end of the egg cup, appear to disappear and show up magically in the large end of the cup. To this day I don't know how he did it.

I thought my father was a great man to be regarded with awe, because he could do that trick. I knew he was a writer, of course, and of some consequence since his picture appeared every day in *The American* with his column, but it did not occur to me that this was more important than his magical powers with the egg.

My father would march back to his room after finishing breakfast with at least four cups of coffee, and again silence would descend on the household unless he called me in for another lecture. This was frequent, since he usually was voluble at that time, being well-fed and filled with news of the day on which he felt moved to make comment.

I attended most of these lectures alone since my sister was sent to a convent when she was ten and I was six. The courses usually ran to blood-and-thunder tales, Old West philosophy, the art and absurdity of war, what every young gambler should know, debating barroom style, editors and censors—how to pull the bull over their eyes.

Some of these lectures were illustrated, others included demonstrations, and frequently the professor felt called upon to inject loud, off-key singing, with much snapping of the fingers, or standing at attention for the military numbers. He was fond of going through the *Manual of Arms* with a shotgun, or saber drill using a cane or other suitable substitute, barking commands to himself. He eventually bought a Civil War cavalry saber for the purpose, although he made a pretense of fancying it as an antique.

This was highly amusing when I was small and merely a spectator, but it was a course of a different color when I was a military academy cadet home on leave. He then insisted on drilling *me* up and down despite my protests that, after all, I got enough of that stuff at school nine months of the year. He finally left off, sadly, as times and military drill changed from the ways he had known.

As I grew older the courses changed. We moved on, for example, to Broadway philosophy, heavily larded with axioms from such eminent authorities as the late Professor Wilson Mizner: Never give a sucker an even break; Professor Runyon: All horse players die broke; anon: How to live with women: Don't.

My father called me into his room for one of his typical talks one day after he'd noted the budding fuzz on my cheek, a variable pitch in my voice and an increasing tendency to notice the ladies underwear ads. He began with much obvious embarrassment.

"Son," he blushed, "it has come time for me to explain a few of the things a young man should know about life. . . ."

"Ah," I interrupted, hoping to save us both from distress, "I a'ready know all about that—er—stuff."

"I was not referring," my father said, "to that—er—stuff. I figured you'd pick up such details around and about, as young fellows do, and you probably know as much or maybe even more on that score than I.

"No," he continued, "that is not the subject I wish to discuss with you, my boy. That kind of—er—stuff you can get from books but such information as the matter I wish to inform you about today is much harder to come by. If you will pay close heed you may save yourself some hospital bills later in life.

"I am going to tell you about the sucker punch."

He explained it also was known as the rabbit punch. He described it as a deadly blow delivered with as much force as possible with the fist on the back of the neck. He said that naturally the success of the sucker punch depended greatly on the element of surprise. He said the trick was to get one's prospective victim to turn his back. He pointed out that only a sucker would do that; hence the name.

Of course (my father said) the sucker punch was strictly against Queensberry and only the lowest form of human life would use it. He wasn't suggesting by his explanation that I ever apply it—only beware of it. He explained it was very dangerous and a fellow could wind up in the jug for life if he used it too effectively.

My father spoke from experience accumulated in his days as a rip-snortin' youth around Colorado and other parts of the West which was called wild, meaning freedom was upon the land, bold men with sixguns kept it, and so did snorting editors who'd steam at intimidation, and a tax collector would have been paid at once with a fast hanging from the nearest arroyo bridge.

My father once had a slight difference of opinion in a saloon with a ham-handed sinister at the bar who suggested they settle the matter outside where there was room for fancy footwork without bowling over any customers. My father accepted, of course, for he would have been ostracized in saloon society had he demurred.

In fact (he said) he turned to go out first with a confident swagger, hoping to demoralize the opposition with his cocksureness. That was his first and last mistake, for the other fellow demonstrated the sucker punch.

My father could hardly turn his head for weeks and no amount of liniment, applied both internally and externally, eased his sore neck. It was no comfort (he recalled) to figure he'd learned one more lesson in the ways of fellow man. The most discomforting part was the fact that he'd played sucker.

He kept upbraiding himself even after the pain in the neck was gone, for he'd been around enough to know the score. He tried to console himself with the thought that you can't go around distrusting everyone in life, but this plea was no good. When you go courtin' trouble (he said) as he did in taking his trade to saloons where the customers debated no-holds-barred, you should be prepared to back up your opinions with force, if necessary, and not be surprised at such tactics as the sucker punch.

My father warned me that if I ever got into an overheated debate and was invited out, I should contrive to get the other fellow to go first. He said not to allow anyone's claim to honesty lure me into easy striking position. He said it was amazing how many fellows who could quote Queensberry to each comma suddenly suffered loss of memory when the stakes were down.

I asked my father why he was so embarrassed telling the lesson of the sucker punch. He explained his red face was due to the follow-up which he felt impelled in honesty to relate to complete the course.

In his next debate which led to an invitation to settle outside, he diplomatically engineered the other fellow out first down the stairs from a second floor bar-and-billiard recreation hall.

His opponent turned out to be heavier in the light of the street than the dark of the saloon. He tried to talk up a peaceful settlement, without appearing to back down, but the other fellow had one of those stubborn, one-track minds.

He dusted the street from one end of town to the other with my father.

This was one of the many lectures my father gave me on health. He suffered hypochondria, becoming alarmed at a sneeze or cough, and his bathroom cabinet had to be opened with caution for it would vomit bottles and tubes of medicine, most of them patent, throat sprays, gargles, cotton, antiseptics and instruments for minor surgery.

He was particularly concerned with the wind instruments of the human anatomy. Even when I was grown he went through a ritual long become familiar whenever he would see me after an absence of some time.

"Stand up," he'd command. I would. He'd close quarters and I'd brace myself. With his fist he'd thump heartily on my chest like it was the gate of heaven. He'd shake his head. "You should take better care of yourself—stop smoking so much." I would always promise, but he knew I wouldn't and I never did.

Not until after he was gone did I learn the reason for this constant medical examination. His father had died of tuberculosis and he, too, once had been a victim. But he never told me these things.

I paid more attention to his courses in journalism and writing. These consisted mostly of generalities —he never specifically explained that "this is the way to write a news story," or "this is the way to spin a fiction yarn." He spent most of his effort teaching me how to learn. His lessons were effective, however, although he was not thoroughly convinced I ever paid any attention.

My father had no religion and I never was able to get from him any commitment on politics. My recollection is that he never voted or, if he did, he kept it a deep secret. The nearest he came to a philosophy was a sort of informal live-and-let-live attitude of the old West.

My mother had a religion, but she was not religious. She went through with the gestures she felt were important and saw to it that my sister and I were drummed through the various major ceremonies in due course. This passing compliance with the religious requisites had its drawbacks, which my parents apparently never learned to foresee.

After my birth they duly fetched me to the fountain for baptism at the Roman Catholic Church of the Ascension at 221 West 107th Street. The priest in command of the ceremony asked what they'd decided to call me. My parents said Damon Runyon Jr. The priest said they couldn't call me Damon. My parents demanded to know why not. Because, he explained, they had to choose the name of a Roman Catholic saint and Damon wasn't one of them.

"Well," my father said, "what is the closest you've got?"

"Damien," the priest replied, after the so-called leper priest who was promoted to saint after his death from the disease. My parents settled for Damien and I was duly doused. They promptly forgot about the compromise and proceeded to call me Damon Jr. The whole incident probably would have remained unknown to me except that in later years I found my birth certificate. I was astonished to learn I wasn't really a Damon or a Junior.

I confronted my father and he told the story to

me. Even if I'd been named Damon I still wouldn't be a Junior. His name was Alfred Damon Runyon. His first name was dropped in writing because the three-word by-line was too difficult to fit in the one column measure of a newspaper using large type.

While my father was not religious he practiced the brotherly love routine more religiously than a lot of rabid churchgoers I have known. He did not get around to thinking about a formal church affiliation until he was doomed with cancer.

My Dear Son:

. . . Sister A——— speaks quite highly of you. I judge that she is a very fine woman and you are to be envied her friendship.

I mentioned to her the fact that one of my own sisters, dead these many years, was a member of her order.

Strange that for a non-Catholic, my sister, who was raised by others after my mother's death, was a Catholic, I twice married Catholics and my children were brought up as Catholics.

I once had some idea of joining the church but after a talk with a priest in Miami it sounded so difficult I did not persist.

In affection,
Dad

Although not a follower of any particular line of religion my father now and then dropped into a church, usually on impulse. These willy-nilly visits were, of course, apart from ceremonies over arrivals, mergers and departures of family and friends.

For his transient churchgoing he usually picked

a Roman Catholic mass because, as he said, "they put on the best show." My father was inclined to express himself in uncommon terms and he meant no disrespect.

Dear Son:

I was much interested in your comments in a previous letter on religion and I am glad you are giving thought to the spiritual phase of existence.

It is something a man has to settle for himself, of course, and while there have been times when I have had some doubts myself, I cannot but feel that faith wrought a miracle for me in my recent illness. As it turned out, it was necessary that I live awhile longer.

I am also glad that you share my thoughts on cities like Cincinnati. A New Yorker has no community life outside of night clubs and they are expensive and tiresome.

You can always visit New York, but you can't always live here in the true sense of living. I notice that most successful writers who are born or migrate here always wind up living in the suburbs or some town outside New York, so I don't see any difference in living far away.

I love Beverly Hills as a small town but of course that's good only if you are in the movie industry somehow. You stick to Cincinnati. You have done well there. Meantime my love to both you and Mary.

Dad

My father had great affection for dumb creatures, human and otherwise. He more often than not had a Neanderthal in training, hock and sometimes in tow, whom he seriously believed to be the coming heavyweight champion of the world. These prospects put so much heart into their eating they never had any left for fighting. There wasn't one who could fight his way out of the subway at rush hour. My father brought one home once, but my mother routed them, shouting, "Get that bum out of here!"

He brought home at least two elephantine hunting dogs that ate like heavyweights and my mother gave them the heave-ho, too. He came in one night with a very small dog, a wirehaired terrier of high breed, and we children were on the verge of winning my mother's nod when the puppy came out of her bedroom chewing what was left of her best shoes.

My father had better success with canary birds. One he brought home, Ernest or Ernie, lived to be so old he couldn't stand on his perch any more and we had to put cotton in the bottom of his cage so he could lie down. My father had more difficulty getting past the door with Pete.

He was gaping into a pet shop window—he couldn't pass one—when he noticed a canary with a bad foot. My father reasoned, rightly, that no one would buy a bird with a game leg and he imagined all sorts of tragic consequences, so he brought Pete home. It developed that Pete was no bargain because he couldn't or wouldn't sing as Ernie did.

My mother stormed at having two birds in the house and predicted Pete would expire from neglect because *she* certainly wasn't going to play nursemaid to a lame canary. She was found sneaking peeks at him during the night, however, and Pete stayed with us until he, too, could stand no longer.

3

My mother was a confounding character. I know her better now after long sober reflection and where I once idolized her through a child's eyes, which were blind to a lot of things, I confess that I since have been forced sadly to take away the pedestal.

Parents are gods to their small children. It is a staggering blow for them to find the gods are mortal, that their power and infallibility are illusions, and that the parents really don't care so much after all.

I was surprised, upon checking my early impressions, to get from my mother's associates such descriptions of her as a "businesslike worker," "a gentle girl," "a wonderful person," "a lovely woman." I had a somewhat, although not entirely different view from my days in back-button britches. My mother also was a tyrant with a hairbrush for a scepter.

She was reared in the accepted manner of her day for producing a lady equipped to run a household, carry on a high-minded drawing room chatter of low content, and snare a likely breadwinner with little more strategy than some coy batting of the eyelashes and perhaps a decorous display of ankle for the more stubborn prey.

This training included diligent attention to the arts which in utilitarian America covered such non-salon activities as cooking and sewing as well as music and art appreciation. The young lady of my mother's time was expected not simply to take a passive interest in these arts, like bending an ear to divas trumpeting in the Denver opera house—she was trained to practice them herself.

My mother's mother was accomplished in everything she put her hand to, whether it was painting or making the Singer sing, for a girl in her day had to be able to do all things. She preferred the art of cooking and I could rattle on about the things grandmother used to make.

My mother could get A in all these activities, but she preferred the drawing room, or even the city room, to the kitchen. Acting was among her accomplishments, but she remained only a spectator in the theatre. She compensated by being on stage in everyday life to the point of making a scene out of a simple greeting to a casual caller.

She never settled for a common hello. She whooped. She cried loudly the praises of the caller if it were someone held in affection or esteem. If she came upon someone she did not like she denounced in the imperious tone of a queen who's been accosted by a common slob. There never was any mistaking where mother stood.

She would share her last bread with any genuine

person, but was death on hypocrites, phoneys and boobs. A hired maid once made off with a costly coat trimmed with caracul. Police tracked the wretch to her lair and at first my mother felt pity and was inclined to plead for her. Then she discovered when the loot was recovered that the unfortunate coatnapper had fancied the trimmings more than the whole coat and had cut off the caracul. My mother's indignation could be heard a block away and she saw to it that the coat butcher got time in city prison to consider her poor taste.

She never forgot a friend no matter how high she moved in life. She used to haul me on long safaris into the wilds of Brooklyn with basket loads of all manner of good things for less successful friends she and my father had known on their way up the ladder. Once she forced a friend to drive us in a consumptive car up rut roads of the Adirondack mountain country to reach a family that had kids all over the place. Who they were or why she went to so much trouble escaped me then and our driver was baffled, too. After one look at the road he wanted to turn back but she yo-ho'd him on with cries of encouragement.

This big-hearted bent was offset by a sharp streak that bordered on cruelty and would have surprised friends who thought she was incapable of such a thing. She was a stern disciplinarian, policing my sister and I with a hairbrush. At times her form of justice smacked of the back room of a Chicago police station. My sister, who was four years older than I, got much the worst of it, but we both suffered stern rearing. My father objected, to no avail of course.

The one time I was delivered to him for punishment he closed the door of his room, presumably so that tortured screams of the damned wouldn't unnerve anyone. While I trembled at the unexpected, he glared fiercely and made stormy noises, all the while popping his razor strop, but finally he broke into a grin and dismissed me with sly winks. He could not bring himself to hit a child.

Thereafter the discipline was left to my mother and she laid on with heavy hand without noticeable improvement over my father's method. Her task was by no means easy and the unwary bystander was in danger of being bowled over by one of us children zooming by in evasive action with my mother in hot pursuit. My sister was at a disadvantage because she had waist-length curls which trailed in her wake and made it easy to check her flight, a device I caught onto at an early age.

The misdeeds that brought on such violent measures were so minor as to be beyond recall. Mother simply was applying one of the rusty saws of the day—spare the rod and spoil the child. The puzzling thing was that she should have known better.

Although slow about it, my mother did come to recognize hospitals, but on some other scores she stubbornly dragged a foot in the past. She was in the vanguard of those who balked at vaccination. "I'm not going to stand for my children being injected with germs and *poisoned*," she cried. "Why, only the other day I heard . . ." She would proceed to give added circulation to some horror story about a child being dispatched by a physician who botched the job. This stand cost her plenty of money since my sister and I had to go to private schools that didn't require vaccination.

She also ignored Edison and persisted in lighting the Christmas tree every year with candles, so the holiday was one long fear of all the family perishing in puffs of smoke. Her struggles to cope gracefully with the booming auto age were monumental and it was only with reluctance that she faced radio. Yet she defied Prohibition with shocking boldness, took up cigarettes just as a gesture of freedom for women, met movies with glad cries, and urged friends to Reno.

My mother was forever trying to polish my father. He reluctantly took dancing lessons but never used them if he could get out of it. A tuxedo was torture to him and he got so he would avoid the house when one of her parties was in full swing. When he was hungry he might forget himself and from his end of the table would come slup-slup sounds over the soup. My mother was a great one for formality and we children were drilled closely in table manners. "Elbows off the table," my mother would command. Some lessons carried implied threats of doom. "Singing at the table brings bad luck."

If my sister and I happened to be in daring mood we might put parental theology to sly test.

"I said stop singing at the table."

"But, Mother, we weren't singing."

"Don't say you weren't singing. I *heard* you. Stop it *immediately!*"

When mother went into high gear on the dramatics she would pull out the stops every few words. Maybe she got into the habit from reading Hearst editorials in which every other word or so was in capital print.

"Mother, we *weren't* singing—we were humming."

"Humming is singing and I want it stopped immediately!"

"But, mother, humming goes like this, Hmm hmm hum hmmm hum, and singing goes like this, Did you ever see a lassie . . ."

Mother's back would go stiff like a ramrod and she would glare. She could glare gavels. One glare from her would have silenced the Senate. Of course we didn't feel it was fair to win an argument with a glare, but then we figured we did good to get as far as we did.

"Do you think we'll have bad luck now?"

"I wouldn't be a *bit* surprised."

Brooding later, my sister and I wondered how one could tell whether a certain stroke of bad luck was due to singing at the table or some other transgression, say, breaking a mirror. We spent a good deal of time on such theological concerns because our parents were surprisingly superstitious.

One stormy day a wind-weary pigeon made a forced landing on our tenth floor window at the Riverside Drive apartment. The exhausted creature tried to huddle in a corner away from the blasts coming in off the Hudson River, but it was about to give up when mother's better instincts got a grip on her. The pigeon was placed in Pete's cage and the two canaries were forced to put up with each other. Mother was onstage, pacing back and forth, doing a melodrama.

"*Why* did this have to happen?" she agonized. "A bird flying in the window means bad luck. Why couldn't that *animal* have picked some other window?" The two small theologians spotted an opening. "But, mother, the bird didn't *fly* in—we took it in. The poor bird . . ." Loud groans from the leading lady. "I tell you this means *bad* luck." She paused to give her audience the day-of-doom look. Silence from the audience, Mary, the hired girl, Ernie, Pete and me—oh, yes, and the new boarder, who was just starting to breath again. "This means," came the announcement in funereal register, "a *death* in the family."

Before she swept off, leaving us to contemplate this curtain speech, she gave us a warning to stymie any childish pleas later. "That bird has got to go," she said, "as soon as it recovers, of course." We were all plunged into dark thoughts. The pigeon, which could hardly turn around in Pete's cage, recovered and was released several days later. Life went on.

About a year later a distant in-law of mother's went six deep, setting mother off again. "I *told* you," she cried to one and all, "I told you so. It was that *bird* that did it. I knew it! I knew it! I knew it!"

Many of my parents' views were originated on the frontier for utility value. Out where the land and the natives were savage, all people were accepted on the basis of what they could do, not who they were, where they came from or who they knew, and the woman's place was in the home. My father wasn't a pioneer like his father, but the pioneer's ideas carried over to his generation.

This may have had something to do with the way our parents' teachings were handed down as dogma. Perhaps dogma had survival value back when little children had to be hushed while the scalp-scouting savage stalked nearby or when a mother had to save wind to make a run for it, as my father's maternal grandmother once did. When there comes an age of reason, however, dogmatic teaching can have severe drawbacks.

"Do as I say," mother would command. Naturally we wanted to learn reasons, so we would ask, "Why?" This was regarded as gross insubordination. "Because," the dogmatist snapped, "*I* said . . ." There was no appeal, no matter how unreasonable the demand. To any dogma there usually are two reactions. One is submission. This was my sister's reaction since she got the worst of it, being broken early. The other reaction is revolt, the course I took.

When I was small I was pudgy-cheeked, plump, almost a slob. Then I went into training under mother's coaching. She and my father both fancied themselves first-rate experts on food and they knew every good restaurant, even in the side-road class, from coast to coast. As an eating coach, however, my mother left something to be desired, namely, quiet. At the table she was a Prussian.

"Eat!" came the command.

"But mother—gee whiz, I'm not hungry."

"I said *eat*—don't argue!"

59

Some years of diplomatic negotiations, consisting mainly of stalling, brought her to the point of such exasperation with me that she was reduced to letting me order, within certain limits, what I wanted to eat. I always ordered the same—lamb chops, which were costly, and mashed potatoes, which were a chore. I figured mother would eventually balk at the expense of time and money. Furthermore, the chops were small, so I didn't have to eat much. In addition there was the inevitable vegetable.

"We must eat the green things that grow above the ground," mother reminded at least once a meal. She was dedicated to spinach. She bought the stuff by the bushel basket.

"Eat up *all* the spinach," mother cried. "It's good for your blood—it's got iron in it."

Vegetables like spinach were brought home in the raw and scrubbed and washed and washed and scrubbed for hours. Despite these measures a bit of dirt usually remained. My teeth would crunch these particles and I thought that was iron.

Mother had the fortune teller fever. She was prey to every crystal ball gazer, palmist, card reader and fly-by-night Nostradamus both known and unknown to the police. If she found a tin-pot tea tavern with a retired waitress mumbling senilities over limp leaves she would rush to the phone to flash a report to friends afflicted with the same weakness for such piffle purveyors.

"This one's *mar*velous! I'm telling you, she had me down to a T. . . ." She subjected Mary to the far-seeing speculations of several of these frauds. One told Mary, "If you ever fell out of an airplane you would land in a haystack." I always feared the women might put some of these divinations to the test. I refused to have my future foretold, preferring to be surprised through life.

My father's superstitions were simpler, most of them common gospel in the sports world, with a few left over from western days. He went pale if a hat was tossed on a bed. This was an old West bit of jitteriness, the point of which, if any, escapes me. If he forgot something and had to return home for it he had a ritual to deal with possible calamitous consequences.

This involved sitting down, counting some mystic number, crossing the feet several times and spitting.

When blossoming beauty began to smooth some of my sister's early teen-age awkwardness she came home on leave from convent with her hair looking as if it had got caught in a sausage-grinder.

"Ye gods," mother sobbed, "what happened to your hair?"

"This," the sophisticate drawled, sashaying around the foyer, the better for all to see, "is a wind-blown bob."

Mother kept sobbing tremolo like a jazz saxophone.

"What have they done," she moaned, "what have they done to my little girl?"

"*They* haven't done anything," Mary said. "I had it done myself."

"Ohhhhhhh!"

"Mother! It's the latest thing! Don't be so old-fashioned!"

But mother was—she still believed in the hair-brush treatment.

I was puzzled by the post facto drama. What was

all the fuss about? The thing was done. How could a wind-blown bob be undone by the hairbrush applied south of the debacle? Besides, shouldn't one be up-to-date, even if the style was atrocious? Didn't many of her set have the same horrible haircuts and wear the latest formless gowns with highballs in their hands?

"Don't gamble," father would warn, turning away from the Saratoga dice table where he'd just dropped $800 in an hour and $10,000 in one month. "All horse players die broke," he announced to the tune of tearing tickets he'd bought on losers. "Don't marry," he'd say after some marital discord. "Watch your lungs," he'd cough over the third daily pack of cigarettes. How was one to figure such advice?

In training me to be a newspaperman and writer my father played long and loud on the chords of kindness. In effect his tune went, "Boost if you knock." If he called a boxer a bum fighter, for example, he would also paint the subject as a nice guy.

But I knew my father personally did not feel kindly toward a number of people whom he privately would not hesitate to label N. G. In one unguarded column he let fly against the expression, "He loves people." Ironically, a writer on his own paper, the *New York Journal-American,* said after my father's death, "He loved people."

My mother, on the other hand, would come right out and announce loudly to whomever it might concern, including the subject, that she would not let fall a tear and might even laugh if so-and-so were stricken with the pox. She was about as subtle as a stomach pump. A child confronted with two such opposite approaches to life can choose one or the other. My sister chose to be kind and never hurt anyone. Life belted her in the face at every turn. I liked my mother's direct approach—and can show scars for it.

In early family days my father frequently took my sister out in her fancy baby carriage and, later, on a sled whenever snow fell on Riverside Drive, but more and more business took him away and the little girl grew lonely for him. It was no help when I came along and what attention there was given to children had to be divided. By the time I was five and she was nine our mother was talking of desperate measures.

During childhood I was assaulted so frequently by aches and ailments, a number of them requiring hospitalization, I got more parental attention than my sister. At one time the doctor decided I needed "iron" and prescribed a tonic. It made me feel right pert. Not until 1953, when I saw a dusty jug of this patent "iron" tonic on a druggist's shelf near the Lydia Pinkham's, did I learn by reading the ingredients that it was nearly all alcohol, stronger than wine. No wonder I felt better! What interested me at that late date was what effect the tonic had toward the making of an alcoholic.

While I was getting so much attention my sister was becoming loud. Nothing specific, no particular crime that could be fingered, just loud. She sang loud, she ran loud, she bounced loud on a bed accompanying herself with a rising and falling, long and loud, "YaaaaahHyaaaaaaHyaaaaaah!" Sometimes she just whooped aimlessly through the apartment.

Nothing first degree—just loud. Her loudness increased with my age and ailments. Heavy applications of the hairbrush seemed to avail nothing except to induce crying, loud.

She was a "bad child." She was loud. Therefore, she was bad. So ran the rule of the day. "I just don't know what I'm going to do with that child," my mother fumed. My father still treated Mary with the grand manner reserved for ladies, small or large, but after all, he wasn't around all day. In fact, he was going farther abroad to "get the money." "The kids are your job," he told my mother.

When Mary was ten (and I was six) my mother announced she was "sending the child away" to learn to be a lady, meaning to quiet her down. This was not the kind of attention my sister was seeking but protests went unheeded. One day my mother, Mary, the hired girl and I went to deposit Mary in the quiet precincts of the Convent of Mount St. Vincent on the Hudson River at Riverdale, which is just across the Harlem River that separates Manhattan from The Bronx.

The institution was set on a high hill overlooking the river and had sprawling green grounds, spotted with holy statuary. Over all was the quiet atmosphere that prevails at the better sanitariums. We went into the great main hall pervaded by gloom and the odor of old incense. Here a stout nun with a firm hand stood ready to receive the little newcomer. The dull, funereal air was pierced by the little girl's cries, sometimes rising to shrieks, that ricocheted off the high ceiling.

"Please, don't send me away, Mother, please don't!

Please don't leave me here! I'll be good, honest I will, Mother, just please don't leave me here! I don't like it here! I want to go home! Please don't send me away!"

The enormity of what was done to my sister struck me silent, solemn and suspicious from that dreadful day forward. She was no louder than any other little child seeking attention and affection or reassurance. I never knew her to do a bad deed. She was, in fact, a gentle, quiet warm-hearted person who never hurt anyone. If the giants would imprison her, for no discernible reason, they would do the same to me. If a loud child was a bad child, to be put away in a dungeon of gloom, then a good child must be a silent child. I became a silent child.

Now the great apartment fell lonely and silent. I had one playmate for awhile until he wrestled me to a marble hall floor and broke a tooth and—I learned years later—my nose. I knew one other boy, distantly. He was a Chinese, son of a King Features Syndicate cartoonist, who lived in the apartment house across the street. From ten stories up we used to converse by shouting when my folks were out. I never met him face to face. Otherwise I played by myself. Silently, of course. I learned to draw and drew praise from my mother. So I drew a lot. She gave me real artist's pencils and paper and the accolade, "Such a good boy—so quiet."

My sister would come home some week-ends, perhaps once a month, and for a time the hired girl and I visited her on the alternate week-ends, but it was a long way by subway and took time, so these visits eventually stopped. As my sister grew up she grew away. Soon when she would come home she preferred dressing up, fixing her hair and posing before mirrors, to playing with me. I was just a child. Then she took to dancing dreamily in the big foyer to "Blue Skies" on the victrola, ignoring me. I felt all alone now.

Mother began to take me on many of her excursions. She and my father, so entirely different from the start, now moved in worlds apart. His was the Broadway-sports sphere. Her crowd included the motion picture set and another group that, like millions of others, didn't take Prohibition seriously.

She didn't disapprove of all sports figures, for many of her friends were high in that field. Her objection was to the "punk" element. While "characters" were my father's stock-in-trade, she didn't think he should bring his work home with him. Where, then, was a guy to go?

He'd had enough woe on that score and it was ironic that my mother would not come to terms— after all, she'd balked at the wedding march until he'd done the never-more act. In Prohibition days there was as much hoisting in the salons as there had been in the saloons and my father wanted no part of either.

While mother had given up reporting for a reporter she still had a drive to see life at first hand, to view the passing scene on the spot, and an overwhelming desire to communicate her impressions to someone. She picked on me.

We would speed to the scene of major news events as soon as the first editions were cried by newsboys.

We raced to Long Island to join a crowd gaping at an ordinary house. In a ghastly whisper my mother informed me that this was where the housewife Ruth Snyder batted .500 against her sleeping husband, using a sashweight, when her sniveling boy friend botched the job.

We dashed to a hotel service entrance where mother pointed to the sidewalk and announced dramatically, "Here is where Arnold Rothstein was found *shot!*" When some Germans crossed the Atlantic in a weird rotor boat, propelled by wind turning two strange pillars, we were at dockside to investigate the newfangled angle. The British brought in an old slave ship once used in the Australian run and we spent a day peeking into tight dungeons and iron maidens.

We went aboard the largest liner, the *Leviathan,* gawked at the tallest building, the Woolworth, and took in every sight worth seeing in New York City. My mother accompanied all these tours with running commentary of her own and pumped guides dry of answers. We made a special trip to Washington and the guides were happy to see us leave.

Not a motion picture or Broadway show escaped us. Although I was only a small boy my mother hauled me to such productions as *Show Boat, The Three Musketeers, Desert Song,* and, among movies, *The Big Parade, The Gold Rush, Don Juan,* and, of course, the first talkie, *The Jazz Singer.*

After we'd see a musical my mother would sit down at her Steinway and rattle off the entire score —by ear, as the saying goes. Her mother had once paid for the usual formal lessons which young ladies took as a natural course, but the teacher gave up after a couple of sessions because my mother already could play everything by ear.

The teacher also was dismayed by her flair for ragging classical compositions. I was once relating her ability to improvise to Professor Eddie Condon, the eminent Greenwich Village jazz maestro, and he observed that such talent was very rare in a woman.

My mother never did anything professionally after marriage with either her reportorial talent or her musical ability except to employ the latter for the entertainment of friends. Nor was she able to find an outlet professionally for her acting, although she had contacts that would have turned a Hollywood aspirant jade.

One of her closest friends in those days was Mabelle Kent, formerly of Denver society, whose husband, Sidney R. Kent, became a lord of the motion picture industry. Mrs. Kent and her daughter, Peggy, Mother, Mary and I spent summers together while the men of the families made fortunes.

It was through the Kents that mother met the motion picture crowd during the days when movies were made around New York City, mostly on Long Island. These friends were the moguls who stayed in the East controlling the industry when the rest moved to California.

We used to go to the studios, great hangar-like places, and watch stars like Norma Talmadge and Adolphe Menjou, then the great lover, make pictures while fiddlers labored out of camera range on mood music. The pictures were silent, of course.

Unions were unknown and mother often joined a

crowd scene or walked through a hotel lobby set. When the picture came to the screen we were at hand to await the great moment. My sister and I would cause a commotion in the theatre by yelling, "There's Mommie! There's Mommie!"

I almost became a child star and escaped only by a hair. Scrubbed to a high gloss, polished and well-combed, I was taken to a studio for a screen test with my howls of protest stifled by a promise of an electric train as part of the salary. I was saved from child labor when the picture potentates decided I was too blonde for the part.

Mother was a nut on photography and packed a camera wherever we traveled. Her photo work showed a flair of boldness which with today's equipment might have made her accomplished at what has become known as photo journalism. She was trying indoor photography and came up with passable pictures back in 1916 with a common box camera and the limited film of that day.

Mother had a fine sense of humor expressed more in action than words. She loved buffoonery and resorted to acting to express her appreciation of the height of the ridiculous. This is a fleeting and difficult thing to commit to paper. Her sense of humor wasn't in what she said, jokes that could be set down, but in what she acted out. She did exaggerated imitations of friends, for example.

One example of her kind of humor was her discovery of the Lady Bird. We were spending the summer at Magnolia, Massachusetts, up the Atlantic coast from Boston, and she came upon the Lady Bird at the amusement park at Revere Beach between

Boston and Magnolia. She came whooping into our rooms at Sadie Kelly's Green Gables and went into a perfect imitation of the barker at the sideshow where the Lady Bird was exhibited: "Hurra, hurra, hurra! Come see the Bird Woman. She looks like a bird! She acts like a bird! She sings like a bird! *She is a bird!*"

Mother was laughing so hard we couldn't quite understand what this was all about. No matter. Nothing would do but we all should pile into the car immediately—Mary, the hired girl and I. Down to Revere Beach we sped. There was the barker, sounding just like mother. She herded us inside, all bewildered since we couldn't imagine what could be so funny.

The inside of the sideshow building was like a round arena such as the one where motorcycle riders circle madly 'round on a wall. In the center of this one, however, was a gigantic cage. Mother kept saying, "She's only a bird in a gilded cage." She was, too. She was the Lady Bird. We stood astounded, gaping open-mouthed, in sort of semi-horror. The Lady Bird was swinging on a trapeze in the middle of the cage. She was sticking out her tongue and making faces at the spectators. Mother could imitate her faces to perfection.

The Lady Bird was a little thing dressed in tights that sprouted tail feathers. She also had feathers sprouting—or attached to her bald head. She had a small wizened face that she could contort as if it were rubber. She just sat swinging back and forth on her perch making faces at the spectators who apparently didn't know whether to laugh or make faces back at her or slink out. Those who laughed and made faces got paid back in kind. As far as I could make out, the Lady Bird was some sort of congenital idiot with a pinhead. This time I didn't laugh along with my mother.

I felt heartsick that an exhibit would be made out of such a pathetic person and I couldn't understand what mother thought was so funny. Perhaps she was laughing along *with* the Lady Bird at the imbeciles roped in by such a hoax. Possibly she was laughing to keep from crying now, because she and my father were so far apart. Perhaps she'd realized they always had been—and always would be.

Thinking back to try to understand what happened to my parents I remember best their rooms at the Riverside apartment and their different ways. I think of my father as leather, real leather with a good creak to it. His room was a small boy's delight. Mexican spurs with large star-pointed prickles that spun around. Whips my father could make lash out and snap. Shotguns of all calibers, some kept broken down and fitted into real leather cases. A curved knife which spoke of the Philippines. A Colt .45 six-gun, the McCoy, long and too heavy for me to handle. His World War I uniform, covered with campaign ribbons dating back to the Spanish-American War. The green arm band with the white C of the war correspondent. A Sam Browne belt. Army compass. Binoculars. Saddle soap. Footballs and baseballs. All the McCoy.

Dominating my mother's room was a gigantic chandelier of cut crystals that jingled with a passing breeze and were a maid's nightmare. The bed was an oversized affair fit for a movie queen. It was painted with Colonial garden scenes and the headboard was tufted. My mother went in for dainty frilled clothes and I remembered most a black taffeta evening gown with huge red roses. The dress went swish-swish-swish which always was a comforting sound to a sleepy child when she would tiptoe in our bedroom to check us while a party was in progress over the rest of the house. Her room was a girl's paradise for my sister and her friends to dress up in playing grown-up.

Years later I came to understand their differences through an incongruous act of my father's. We would be talking, just the two of us, perhaps in a swank suite at the Mayflower Hotel in Washington, and my father would punctuate his remarks with a typical "wild West" gesture. He would spit on the floor. I would say nothing, accepting it as if it were perfectly normal, but I often wondered. A little research showed that to his kind, that wild westerner with the six-gun and the courteous airs, there was nothing wrong with the gesture.

My mother was from the transition stage where the frontiersmen were sitting back to enjoy what they'd made out of the land cleared of wilderness and savages, and were establishing a new culture with different manners. She was in the vanguard of women who were stepping out into the business world to challenge men on their own grounds, while he thought their place still was in the home. He changed later, of course, but then it was too late. She did not wait for him to come home.

She first began acting strangely along about 1922–23 when bathtubs throughout the republic were being ruined by bad gin. Her puzzling conduct was not constant then but occasional, usually when there were gay parties among the summer resort set she met at Haines Falls in the Catskills and Paul Smiths in the Adirondacks where she rented a cottage every year.

Each summer we went through the same routine. The apartment furniture was covered with light slips, Oriental carpets were rolled up and replaced by grass rugs, trunks were packed, and one morning at five o'clock everyone except father, including the birds, piled into the Wills Sainte Claire for the trip to the mountains. Each summer the auto started balking on rugged Route Nine before we'd gone fifty miles, and each time we had to turn back and start anew the next day. The few garages and filling stations along the way did not cater to the Wills Sainte Claire.

The reason we went to all this trouble was because two members of the family, the canaries Ernie and Pete, were not allowed on trains. One year my mother tried smuggling them up in a drawing room where they were hidden under piles of clothing, which almost proved fatal. Every time the porter or conductor came to the door we would all set up loud babble to cover Ernie's protests. Mother decided that was too much trouble and one year tried smuggling the birds aboard the Albany night boat which also carried the Wills to cut the journey to the mountains by road. The morning we docked, however, Ernie greeted the dawn with trilling that could be heard in the early quiet all over downtown Albany.

My mother knew absolutely nothing about the auto except the rudimentary motions of driving and we were frequently stranded helpless on the road when the Wills developed gas pains or some other mysterious ailment, usually miles from nowhere.

When the Wills started coughing mother's only remedy was wheedling. "Willy, Willy, Willy." Everyone would rock back and forth in an effort to help the car along. This was considered especially effective on mountain upgrades, where Willy was most likely to get discouraged. Someone always had to be alert to pull the emergency brake, because it was all Mother could do to keep the car on the road. It was a tall, heavy car with a steering wheel so thick her hands couldn't completely grasp it.

Her top speed was thirty miles an hour and the journey to the mountains took at least fifteen hours, barring breakdowns and blowouts. We started going to the upstate hills because Mother was lonesome for the mountains back home in Colorado. I remember Haines Falls in the Catskills principally because I ran into the road in front of the cottage one day and was clawed by a Stutz Bearcat. I was bowled over and torn up by the gravel road but no bones were broken since the Bearcat was just crawling.

This was the second time I was "run over"—the first was at four years at Riverside Drive and 95th Street—because Mother didn't teach us how to cross streets. In fact, most of our troubles could be traced to lack of knowledge—what we didn't know hurt us.

74

This applied especially to my mother's sudden change in conduct. She would act silly, or make seemingly incoherent statements, or fawn over us with evil-smelling breath, or teeter. If we asked what was wrong she would grab her bosom, roll her eyes and groan dramatically, "Oh, my poor heart. I'm not well." Soon she was not well a good deal of the time. Her fits of ill health became more frequent as the years—and parties—went by.

One night in the apartment on Riverside Drive my sister awakened me with fearful whispers. "Mother," she hissed, "is lying on the floor in Daddy's study. What'll we do?" Clinging to each other, trembling in the silent and dim-lit apartment, we went to investigate. We tiptoed into the big foyer and then edged into the long living room to a point where we could just see through the open French door into the dark study. The only light was in the foyer back of us so we could barely make out the form of mother's fur coat on the study floor. "Oh, Lordy," Mary gasped, her voice quavering, "do you suppose she's dead?"

I was so scared I didn't dare speculate. "Go see," I urged her, giving a slight push. "You come with me," she insisted. We inched along. "You go first," I whispered, "you're the oldest." We weren't getting very far fast. Mary pulled herself together. "No use being scaredy cats," she said, more to herself than to me. She barged forward and gave a closer look from the study doorsill. "Why," she sighed, "the coat's empty." Our relief was only momentary. Where, then, was mother? We tiptoed back to her bedroom after deciding not to wake the hired girl in the servant's quarters off the kitchen. Mother was sleeping soundly. She'd dropped her coat on the floor when she'd come home. That wasn't like her.

By 1928 I long had known what was wrong with mother. Not that anyone told me. A child, of course, didn't notice such things, so I had to put one and one together for myself when mother took me on ventures such as parties at a big Southern-style mansion owned by wealthy friends in Westport, Connecticut. One night there mother was helped into bed beside me and I heard her women friends laughing that she'd "had too much." I lay trembling all night long listening to her heavy breathing, afraid it would stop. She was getting out of control and it was a fearful experience when one of the giants got out of control.

That summer we stayed home. My father was stricken with appendicitis and then pneumonia. While he was recuperating at home, with my mother as chief nurse, we came to grips with the radio age just abornin' with howls and squeals.

A man delivered the infernal machine and a lecture on how to work it. A corner of the study was allotted since a pile of batteries, wet and dry, were required to operate it. The vitals were in a box more than two feet long and one foot wide, eight inches tall, with three big dials and two smaller knobs that had to be adjusted just right. On top stood a tall loudspeaker resembling a huge inverted ear trumpet. These main parts were finished in crinkled hideous brown. Aerial and ground wires were required and everyone was warned away from the batteries hidden behind a tall chair. By adroit fiddling with the dials we got weird noises vaguely identifiable as the Democrats in national convention.

My father tried relaxing by the radio but it was as unpredictable as "Willy" and much time was spent running for the repairman at the corner on Broadway. The thing so exasperated my father he never again attempted to learn how to dial a radio even when the trick could be done with the flick of one knob. Besides, more serious matters were attracting his attention elsewhere. Evidently my mother's gallivanting around had come to his notice, although he'd been doing some himself. In fact, mother knew about it.

My father stomped into managing editor Gene Fowler's office at the *New York American* and point-blank accused his old friend of telling mother he was running around with another woman. Fowler was deeply hurt—the accusation was untrue—but the amiable giant tried to placate my father. He, however, fumed in rage, "I think I'll go out and get good and drunk." Fowler was alarmed. "Damon," he argued, "you can't do that—it would be the worst thing you could do and wouldn't solve anything." He put aside the unjust accusation and his own feelings to talk my father out of turning to drink.

Undoubtedly my mother had charged my father with breaching his vows. The hours he worked and the beat he covered had something to do with his dallying. When he finished work the inclination was to relax, but where the so-called "average man" flings himself on the living room couch for a fast snooze or at worst stops for a few with the boys at 5:30 P.M., my father wasn't done with work until around 3 A.M. and his crowd did their relaxing at the tight little night spots where the chorines were costumed (to use the word lightly) to keep the customers awake.

It was 1928, the height of the Prohibition era, when the big blow-off came. I was the only other person home when my father and mother went into a door-slamming debate that finally exploded out of his room. I cringed to one side, petrified with fright at the mysterious shaking of my small world.

As my father led the storm across the hallway to my mother's room, even a child could tell he was furious and she was on the defensive. He had brought charges, which she denied completely, and I was to learn later that what really burned him up was her attempt at deception on a subject in which he was expert. He was going to prove his charge. He flung open her closet door and simply pointed. On her closet shelf my mother had tucked away a bottle. Without another word he went and packed his bags.

He went to another woman.

My mother began to destroy herself. It is a slow, untidy process by the jug route. She and I moved to Bronxville, a suburb of New York City, with an Irish girl who stuck by her.

My sister stayed at convent—she'd had enough. My father came home only once when mother insisted he attend a Boy Scout father-son affair. She threatened to go to the city and fetch him if he didn't show voluntarily. He knew she would, too.

My mother was always "sick" now, spending most of her time in bed at home. I feared my playmates would find out and went through inner agonies whenever one came to the door or inquired about her. I had friends in only when she was out. Several times when she was "sick" some of the boys happened by, as on Halloween night, and she made a valiant effort to straighten up and play the gracious hostess. If the boys noticed anything amiss they said nothing and I got them out as soon as possible.

She was in bad shape. Liquor hits a woman hard and fast. Some men can guzzle day in day out a score of years before it hits them, but a woman is shot in five years or less. My mother looked fifteen years older than she was. She slopped around and got maudlin. A woman's legs usually go bad, too, and she stumbles and falls.

The last time we went for the summer to Lake Placid, where we had a cottage at the Stevens Hotel, there were several messy scenes where my mother had to be helped home by my sister and the hired girl who then were hard put to keep her there quietly. We took a cruise to Bermuda and mother couldn't even get off the boat most of the time we were there. That time she was "seasick."

Such soft terms as "sick" were used to deceive me. It's beyond me how people could believe I didn't know the real reason for mother's condition, especially since I was the one with her on earlier parties and excursions.

I'd been playing along with the family act and pretending I didn't notice anything unusual—although I hadn't the faintest idea why all the pretense—but now it was getting impossible to keep up such a farce. Mother didn't go out much any more—she just took to bed and bottle.

The summer of 1931 we had the huge home of a General Motors executive at Rehoboth Beach, Delaware. One day my sister, now getting to be quite a lady, said to me: "Let's take a walk up the beach." The sand stretched for miles and we walked a way in silence before stopping to sit. Mary said, "I think it's about time you should know what's wrong with mother, why she's been sick all these years." Before she could go on I said, "I already know." Mary looked incredulous. "Sure," I said, "she drinks too much." Mary cried, "What? Do you mean to say you've known that all along?" I nodded. I suddenly felt very sorry for Mary and others who went to such great lengths acting all those years. But then I'd done a little acting myself.

We discussed our parents and their strange ways. "What makes me so mad," Mary fumed, "is that they don't *do* something. That nobody *does* anything. Why don't they get a divorce and have it over with? But no, they just keep on this way. They are married and they aren't married. Why doesn't someone *do* something with mother? She can't go on like this. She ought to be made to quit drinking—or something. I don't know what. But nobody *does* anything." She threw a handful of sand into the wind in a gesture of futility.

My sister was on our father's side. She blamed mother, who she thought should have had enough gumption to fight. I blamed my father, believing he had walked out when the going got rough, taking with him my mother's will to live. Even when we were grown my sister and I usually wound up shouting over this question. Eventually we came to the point where we hardly ever discussed it any more.

Still treated top secret, where I was concerned, were the Broadway shenanigans of my father. This attitude was so short-sighted and patently silly, even to a child, that it irked me into everlasting detestation of the asinine artifices of censorship.

Mother was inclined to get loud when airing her woes to close friends and my young radar ears picked up more, perhaps, than was good for me. Once in the city mother ordered the chauffeur to halt and dispatched the Irish girl to investigate an eyesore-yellow roadster at the curb. When the scout returned I heard this "guarded" conversation:

"Was it her?" my mother inquired darkly.

"Yes, she was in an auction room."

I would have had to have been deaf, dumb and blind for the significance to escape me, since my father had sent the same jaundice-colored car to Bronxville to carry friends and me to the circus. I would have had to have been made of stone to ignore the effect all this had on my mother.

Every morning now when I would be going to school at Bronxville my mother would call to me from her room. "I just want to see you," she'd say. I didn't want to see her. I didn't want to see her destroy herself. I would stand at the door. The room reeked of bad booze. Then I would leave heartsick. November 4, 1931, I met her in the little second floor hallway. The hired girl was helping her back to her room. She wavered there in her night clothes, squinting at me, crying, "Let me see you! I might not be here when you get back. All the Egans die on November the fourth." She babbled a list.

I wanted to get out and away. "Don't be silly," I said. "Nothing's going to happen to you." I broke away and fled to school, trying not to think about it. As it turned out she was wrong by five days. November 9, soberly and calmly, she suddenly said to her companion, "Get the priest." The girl didn't stop to question but ran a block to fetch the priest.

Then the girl tried to get the doctor who had attended mother for years and, I think, probably was in love with her although both were married and had families. For the first time he refused to come. "It's no use," he said. "I can't do anything for her. She doesn't want anyone to do anything for her. She just doesn't care any more. I can't save her. I wish to God I could, but I can't and no one else can either."

My mother was clear-headed and calm when the priest left. In fact she seemed to have taken some turn for the better, and her companion thought everything was going to be all right. My mother smiled and whispered, "Don't worry." She turned her head toward the window by the bed and closed her eyes.

A kid yelled to me across the street in the school ground, "Yer father's home!" I didn't go at once for that clearly was ridiculous. It must be the doctor.

But as I walked the small path to the attached house we rented I felt what believers in such matters would call a premonition. I looked up at the second floor bedroom window to see if the shades were drawn. They weren't, but my father *was* home and so were all my mother's closest friends, whom we hadn't seen for a long time, packed into the little sitting room.

82

If anyone gave an explanation I don't recall it and it wasn't necessary nor possible for I was loudly lamenting in the dining room and could hear a basket bumping down the stairs. I kept wondering why they hadn't drawn the shades, the way movies and books reported.

Later I snuffled upstairs with my father to my room to discuss plans. All of a sudden he put his head on his arms on a table and for the first time I heard a man cry. It stopped me.

At the time of my mother's death my father was living in a small penthouse atop the Hotel Forrest on West 49th Street between Broadway and Eighth Avenue, center of the area which he used as the locale of most of his "guys and dolls" stories. He had no room for us, Mary and I, so we were sent to Washington to live with my mother's sister and her family, including our grandmother Mamie.

"You," my aunt told me in later years, "were the lonesomest little boy in the world. You wouldn't talk to anyone. Everyone tried to be friendly and draw you out but you stayed all within yourself." I was so quiet I finally was taken to a child expert who prescribed "a lot of ice cream sodas." The idea seemed to be that I was grief-stricken and that I would get over it. Meanwhile, I should be left alone. I didn't need any special treatment because there wasn't anything wrong with me.

My own feeling was perfectly clear to me. The nearest person to me was gone and I knew no one would care as much again even if he wanted to and tried. I knew my father, aunt and family meant well, but that I was a stranger who could never be accepted completely. The fine difference was sensed as only children can sense such vagaries in life. I simply tried to stay out of the way as much as possible, pending the time when I could take care of myself. Of course I was lonely—a terrible void inside—but I was conditioning, or adapting, myself to accept that way of life. I accepted rejection.

My sister and I both felt rejected by our father. We understood perfectly why this was so, and we knew he didn't mean to reject or was unaware that he was rejecting us. This was plain fact. He had a profitable way of life which he enjoyed and obviously didn't want to give up to provide a home for us. Besides, he remarried in 1932. My sister married, too, and left our home in Washington.

I was going to a parochial school with a semimilitary curriculum—that is, there was close order drill three days a week and the boys wore gaudy uniforms of Southern gray and maroon. My father somehow found out that my class was ruled with iron hand. Although I was so quiet the attentions of a child expert were thought necessary, even I got smacked across the face and had my hair pulled several times by teachers. My father was furious, a commentary on his views of my mother's form of punishment. He withdrew me immediately. "If I'd known they would hit you at that school," he apologized, "I'd never have let you go there in the first place." Of course my aunt didn't know either since she was never able to get any comment out of me.

My father and his new wife moved into an elaborate penthouse at the Parc Vendome on West 57th Street and he and I discussed schools. It was understood, of course, that I would go away to school. I simply accepted the fact without feeling rejected because I'd already assumed the rejection. He suggested some fancy prep school like Andover or Exeter. He had visions of sending me to Yale or Princeton or Harvard. We went so far as to look at Andover, but I knew I was no scholar nor the blazer type. The discussion turned to military schools until the only question was, which one?

The night Zangara took a shot at Franklin D. Roosevelt, missed and hit Mayor Cermack of Chicago in Miami, my father was a couple of blocks away admiring the marching style of the sixty-piece band from Riverside Military Academy, which had winter quarters at Hollywood, eighteen miles north of Miami. The school's main base was Gainesville, Georgia.

I liked the idea of Riverside since it was the number one honor school in the R.O.T.C. system. My father pointed out that he wintered in Florida and I could come home week-ends. He gave me an explanation of why he wanted me to go away to school. "I want," he intoned, "for you to meet boys from all over, different parts of the country, to learn to get along with everyone. I also want you to learn to say 'Yes, sir,' and 'Yes, ma'am,' instead of 'Huh.'" I looked at him to see if he was leveling with me. "Yes, sir," I said.

4

From the day I went to live with my father there was tension in the family air since both of us were inclined to be bluntly vocal.

He seemed to feel I did not admire his Broadway life, and he was right. I didn't realize then, of course, that my attitudes toward him in those first awkward days were conditioned by my mother.

From the moment he assumed command of our household immediately after her death I looked upon him as a stranger and an intruder. I took a dim view of his motives. Although I never said anything I was not able to keep from looking what I felt.

He consulted Mary and me on plans for a tall tombstone to mark the Runyon plot in Woodlawn. I considered his heavy expenditure merely marble salve for his conscience, which I assured myself must be hurting fiercely. I shrugged. "It's O. K." Children can be almost as cruel as adults.

It wasn't until long later that I learned and came

to appreciate fully that he really was stunned by what had happened to the once gay girl he had shyly courted as if reaching for a star. Her sudden death was the one solution he hadn't expected in their domestic trials. He always made sure her grave was kept covered with the flowers she had loved.

My first explosion over this stranger in our midst came when the family in Washington, using the gentle tact usually reserved for deaths, broke the news that my father had married again shortly after mother's death. I raged so feverishly they feared the consequences when I was sent to live with my father and his new wife.

Actually inside I was sick with fear and anxiety. The terrible picture of my sister's incarceration in the convent as a child remained to haunt me. I was just hoping that wherever I was sent wouldn't be quite as doomy. I remained the solemn, silent, suspicious child of yesteryear. So did he, with blundering results.

His shy overtures of friendliness, his stumbling attempt to play the palsey Pop, were so patently gawky that I figured then that he was only going at it half-heartedly as a dull chore forced upon him by circumstances. I began to evade rather than try to understand. Yet there were moments of closeness.

These usually came when he would resort again to the lectures he had given me when I was small. He seemed to be one of those parents who was at his best with a child too young to present an aggressive personality that might clash with his. He was not receptive to exchange in conversation. So I listened or pressed questions to keep him going. I had the feeling one had to be patient with such a character.

Some of his lectures appeared to have little or no practical application. He would give detailed descriptions and comments on individual boxers through the history of fisticuffs. These lectures were accompanied by demonstrations.

"John L. Sullivan," he'd announce, solemnly striking a tableau pose, standing stiffly braced with fists cocked in the awkward style of the tintype era of boxing. He'd shift a foot and fist, then announce, "James J. Corbett." Not daring to laugh, I'd view all this with straight face.

Whenever he'd take me around in his sports circles—say to the office of ticket broker and later fight promoter Mike Jacobs—I'd hear him argue for the umpteenth time some controversy considered serious among sporting people, such as did or didn't Jack Johnson really get knocked out in Havana?

Most of these debates struck me as absurd since either side was unprovable. There was always the old one of whether Jack Dempsey could have beaten Joe Louis. It seemed silly since each fought under different circumstances and rules. Besides, I'd wonder, what difference did it make?

My father held a nebulous position in the promotion of heavyweight title bouts. In certain cases he represented the Hearst Milk Fund for Babies, a pet project of Mrs. William Randolph Hearst, Sr. In others I never was sure where he stood. His lecture on the Louis style was the only one that proved of some practical value.

His definition of the Louis plan went something like this: Joe fought standing straight, with his left shoulder hunched so his glass chin was hard to reach, and he always kept moving to the left to make it difficult to swing a right on him.

At a beer brawl years later in a one-room Washington apartment I became embroiled with a drunken Texas oil wildcatter, who topped me by a head and maybe a hundred pounds. I took exception to his familiarity with the doll I was escorting, although she'd put me on the spot by failing to heed danger signals.

The clod rushed me with a roar and I barely had time to whisk off my glasses. All my father's lectures on boxing flashed back. Since I weighed little more than a Thomas Wolfe novel I knew I had to stay clear of the heavier fellow or I'd be gone in the clinches.

"Keep moving to the left" ran through my head and I concentrated on cutting up his face. We wound up on the floor, smashing furniture, and I was ducking the sucker punch by the time he was hauled away bleeding. For once I gave silent thanks for my father's lectures. Of course it was all around town the next day that I'd been boozed up although for once that wasn't entirely true. I was clear-headed enough to swear never again to defend a doll who'd mismatch a guy.

My father always was casting dark hints about the temptations of the softer flesh, but I paid no heed, to my regret. He once made a zigzag approach to the bare facts of life, but his manner was so distressed I stifled my curiosity to find out what he really knew about women.

"I know all about that," I said. Since I was thirteen at the time, he was startled at this news. "Really? How do you know? Where did you find out?" I explained patiently, "We were taught all that in biology at Bronxville school." It was a revelation to him that progressive education had come to pass. It was also a relief.

As shy as I was I was downright bold compared to him. He would always ask me to leave when he was taking a shower. He was equally respectful of my privacy. His shyness extended even to his deathbed when he refused to allow the nurse to remove his plates before he entered the blackness of coma.

He always reddened visibly when he was introduced at a public place and more than once I heard him request night club masters of ceremonies to ignore him. At other times, however, he got juvenile delight out of public attention. He seemed to enjoy notice, if the public was at a distance.

He built a modest mansion—all white even to his typewriter—on Hibiscus Island in Miami's Biscayne Bay. On neighboring Palm Island the infamous Al Capone had taken a pretentious home which was pointed out as one of the sights of the Miami scene.

As sightseeing boats toured around these islands the spielers would call attention of the rubbernecks to the various homes of the famous. "Now on your left is the home of Damon Runyon. . . ." Whenever my father would hear the load of rubes chuffing near he'd dash to the patio fronting on the water.

By the time the boat hove in sight the famous author would be reclining in a deck chair. When the spieler could be heard across the water pointing him out my father would wave at the gaping crowd.

They'd all wave back. This bit of by-play never failed to amuse him. Generally his approach to fame was more confusing than amusing as far as I was concerned, however.

He seemed to convey the impression that he felt it was somehow dishonest to take advantage of the weight of fame. He usually insisted on paying his way even when he didn't have to and he warned me against taking advantage. This was a peculiar attitude in a society that dotes on the advantages that go with the spotlight.

The result was that I always was touchy about using *the name* until I evolved a policy of my own in later years. The name haunted me through life as a constant irritant along with the query, "Are you following in your father's footsteps?" My father never taught me how to handle the name because he didn't know there was a problem.

I confused using the name with his lectures about uncompromising honesty as a member of the fourth estate, the profession of which he was so proud. "Never," he cautioned, "let anyone buy you." His earliest lessons included warnings that as a reporter, who probably would need every cent I could get, I might be approached with shady offers. He was right, but fortunately I'd absorbed those lessons.

Yet, again, his attitude on this score was bewildering when you tried to reconcile his ethics with those of some of the circles in which he moved, where more than one deal reeked. I gathered that his insistence was on personal incorruptibility—never mind what the crowd about you is doing.

My father's whole approach to life, including family, was the same as his fictional counterpart in his short stories, the anonymous narrator "I," who attempted to remain the detached observer of the passing crowd. Even when I became engaged, for example, he just sat back to see what would happen. He was the same with others, who were puzzled no end by him.

At home in New York the routine was almost invariable. He arose at noon, groused, lectured, breakfasted, dressed the same as he had when we had lived on Riverside Drive. Then he either worked or went out to view the passing scene. I never knew him to do much else and all the family had to center their activities around his. The day all depended on what he felt like doing. Sometimes he would stick his head in my door and say, "Come on."

If he ever had any particular itinerary in mind he never let on. I'd just lope along beside him and wonder, inwardly meek, where we were headed. He'd suddenly turn into some of the oddest places, such as a tiny shoe shine shop, and start conversing with an old acquaintance, maybe a bootblack.

Frequently he'd head for the Mike Jacobs ticket office, across the street from the Forrest Hotel, and stand around talking and debating with the boys. He nicknamed the street in front of the small Jacobs office Jacobs Beach, because the boys got the sun while standing there. Actually he was working most of the time, for he'd pick up material for his column from these ventures.

Or he might gather the substance of a "guys and dolls" short story. The column and the stories, his work, dominated the life of the entire household sometimes to the point of utter boredom for everyone except himself. At times I'd try to think of some fast excuse for not coming, at the risk of provoking a stormy mood.

For he was subject to weatherlike changes in mood. Literally he could be jovial one minute and glowering the next, depending on whether things went his way. Aside from keeping everyone on the brink of fantods, this king-of-the-hill attitude had an especially disastrous effect on me.

Childlike, I naturally gaped up to my father and tried hard to mold myself in his image. If the herd would snuffle and scuffle around him, as if kowtowing before some god, then it would be for me to try to ape him. If a glower would make people leap with fear, why then I would glower. If he was the center of his universe, then I would be the center of mine. In short, I was trying to follow in father's footsteps without realizing it. It never was a happy choice for me or anyone around me. In some places it was impossible to follow his footsteps.

My father was a dude. He had closets jammed with expensive, tailor-made suits, and shelves full of shoes, perhaps a score and not the forty often credited to him. It took him an hour to find the right combination to wear and he frequently would change two or three times while dressing. He had drawers full of shirts, all tailor-made, and at least a hundred costly ties.

In my early teens my father would announce that we all would eat out at, say, the Colony, a super-swank diner for the Astors and Vanderbilts and such. When I presented myself, scrubbed to a shine, my father would look me over skeptically and ask, "Is that the best suit you've got?" I could only nod dumbly. "Well," he would sigh, "all right, come on."

I became a perfectionist. A small spot on a suit was enough to make me feel as if I'd just climbed out of a muddy gutter and I'd balk at going anywhere. This only brought on a storm. "You're just sulking," my father would glower. "Now cut it out and come on." The storm blew worse when my churning innards led me to order meagerly in a de luxe restaurant. My father would growl. "You can't order just a hamburger in a joint like this. Get a steak or something like that and stop sulking."

I never got up enough courage to point out to him that he was supposed to supply my clothes and that if they didn't look right I hardly could be blamed. What hurt then, however, was not the failure to provide the tangible things, but the apparent disapproval implied. This inner fear of my father was based on intangibles—he personally never gave me any reason to dread him. Most of my fears were vagaries foisted on me by the women of the house warning, "Don't upset your father."

Years later when I was out working myself it suddenly struck me as amusing, in an asinine way, that the women had demanded churchly silence, the better for my father to work. For of course he was accustomed to writing in the bedlam of a newspaper office or at a stadium with 50,000 people yelling in his ear.

I was only too glad to escape the strict atmosphere of home for school, where the rules at least were written with some degree of sense for all and favored none.

For three years, six months I went to Riverside, going up in my military grades and rank—and down in academic grades. I used to get from home what we called poison pen letters denouncing me for low grades. Actually they weren't so bad. I surprised myself by a near perfect record one year in geometry. Years later it developed that I had a knack for scientific subjects in the creative realm, such as theoretical physics, and might have done well in such fields. I made 100 almost consistently in military science and tactics. The poison pen letters got tougher.

Discipline at home got tougher, too. Cadets always leaped at the opportunity for a day or weekend leave since the regime was strict, with a book of rules covering every possible breach of conduct, from "dust on shoes" to "gross insubordination." Several of my friends went home with me for a day or week-end at the house on Hibiscus Island at Miami Beach but they politely rejected a second invitation, pleading "no offense." One told me, "There are more rules at your house than at Riverside."

I was among six cadet officers skipped over the third year to the fourth in military science because of a lack of seniors with sufficient rank from the year before to be promoted into the top brackets, cadet major and captains. We had to cram to make those ranks, all awarded on merit. I was supposed to be a cadet captain commanding a company and this was important because our records went to the

War Department if we were commissioned second lieutenants in the reserves.

While cramming on military subjects for paper examinations the beginning of my fourth year I let my academic subjects slide until after permanent ranks were conferred. The poison pen letters got worse. Just before I went into the paper examination where I would be weakest I got a letter from my father threatening to take me out of Riverside the next week if my grades didn't improve instantly.

I was the only one who wasn't surprised when I didn't "make captain." In an unusual move, since all the military orders were treated with high secrecy apparently for training purposes, the regular Army Captain who was Professor of Military Science & Tactics broke the bad news before the permanent ranks were read to the battalion. I was to be highest ranking first lieutenant, just below the lowest ranking Captain.

"We checked and rechecked all your grades over and over from every angle," the PMS&T told me, "and you missed by just a tiny fraction. But we couldn't make up that fraction. What happened?" I told him, but of course the grades stood. The system was worked out by the War Department and there was no hedging. Now the whole thing seems trivial, but it was the kind of blow that sinks teen-agers. It also changed my life.

I proceeded to be the best cadet officer I could be, but I spent every night in study hall for low academic grades. I just didn't care any more and I spent that Christmas in Atlanta with my roommate. The reason I worked so hard at the military side of school life was so the corps wouldn't think I was a "sore-head" for losing out. I couldn't very well explain to 750 cadets, most of them total strangers.

In the sixth month of my fourth year, March 1937, my platoon won a close order drill competition with a performance that made one of the regular Army officers remark, "That's the best I've seen since West Point." There was a reason. I'd told the platoon I was leaving school and wanted to win to show that I hadn't deliberately let down. The performance got me the first military efficiency medal awarded a cadet officer of my rank.

This was pinned on at a formal parade Sunday when 10,000 spectators would flock to see the drill. The commandant told me the night before that he'd personally phoned my father to tell him to be there. He didn't come. That week I had consultations with faculty officers for their private judgment. I explained I planned to go into the newspaper business and that I didn't feel I could learn any more at school. "Under the circumstances," one said, "you probably couldn't get any more out of school and you'd probably be better off leaving."

I asked my father to come up on Wednesday, a "town leave day," alone. He did and I told him I was leaving. I didn't say I wanted to—I was leaving. He took it with amazing calm. "You don't have to go to Riverside," he said. "You can pick out any school in the United States and go to it. You can go to any college you want, but you should finish school." I didn't even think it over. "No, thanks," I said.

"You understand," he said carefully, "that once you leave home there's no turning back. I will give you the best education I can afford but after that you're on your own." Understood. He asked, "What will you do?" I pointed out that my sister was going to Cleveland with her husband and child. She'd offered to take me with her. "I'll go into the newspaper business, of course," I said.

"You'll starve."

"No, I won't. I'll make a million dollars."

"You'll starve. Prepare to starve for ten years."

"All right, I'll starve for ten years, but I'm going."

"Well, you're free to do what you please, only— only I wish you'd finish school first."

"I've made up my mind and I'm not going to change it. I've thought, and thought, and thought, and this is it."

"Any school in the United States. Any place you choose, where you think you'd be happy, and there'll be no more of those letters from home."

"It's a little late to think about that."

My father and I looked at each other across the years, strangers. What did he think a son wanted? I knew he could not understand, and I wasn't going to try to tell him. He wanted his own life—and mine, too. He could have his.

In two weeks I was working for United Press in Cleveland. My father dropped into town several times and and it always amused me to see the veteran Hearst man bewildered and unnoticed in the rival Scripps-Howard's *Cleveland Press* city room looking for me. Once I received a telegram from the Hearst desk in New York asking if he was in Cleveland. I wired back: "Hearst's Runyon unshows here. (signed) Scripps-Howard's Runyon." It pleased him. On his visits he always looked at me with a bemused air of wonderment. I wasn't starving.

My father was always working even when he was just visiting me in Cleveland where he had no story to do. Now that I was out working myself I could understand this a little better than when I was a child. I realized that even when he was sitting and talking about this and that he was working. This is true of members of the professions—science, including medicine, the arts and journalism—which is why so many of them are no bargains as spouses or parents.

It's difficult if not impossible for the non-professional to understand that a writer, for example, may be working even when he's just staring out a window, because the work is mental and not merely the act of punching typewriter keys. All my father and I ever did when we visited together was sit or walk. We talked, but often we were silent for long stretches of time. We never discussed family or related problems. After a few preliminaries of the how-have-you-been variety our talk turned to the life going on about us.

In Cleveland we stood in the Public Square and observed pigeons and people who feed them. Why do people go out of their way to fill the bellies of the beggar birds? Like that ragged old man—he looks like he could stand a few bags of popcorn himself. Are such people just lonely? Aren't we all? We watched the rush hour crowd fight home from work.

Where did they go? Why were they in such a hurry? What did they do when they got home? What did they think and talk about?

In Washington we sat in the railroad terminal—stations were especially interesting places to sit—and watched and discussed the travelers. "That dyed blonde in the mink coat," my father would say, "is not Washington. She is not just coming home."

I agreed. "She's overdone, too conspicuous for Washington. Looks more like New York."

"She's not a show girl. She would be wearing dark glasses and more make-up. But she's New York, all right."

"She knows where she's going. She headed right for the cab exit. She's been here before."

"But where's her luggage—oh, the porter there, the one with the little overnight bag. She must have money or she'd carry it herself."

"That means she isn't going to stay long."

"You can bet," my father offered, "that she is not visiting home."

All this was work—some day we might use such observations in a story.

My father was an agony writer. That is, writing was heavy labor for him and each word hit the paper bathed in sweat. Writers vary in this respect. At the other extreme, according to legend, was Heywood Broun. It's said he used to knock out his daily column of 700-odd words in thirty minutes or less.

My father thought his whole story out long in advance so the actual writing was a mechanical process of polishing and retouching. For his short stories he resorted to longhand to write the first draft, sometimes doing this chore in bed, a way of working fancied by Mark Twain. The final draft was the result of several rewriting sessions at the typewriter.

It was heavy going not only for him but for the rest of us around the house since he became more moody than ever and was difficult if not impossible to deal with during these periods. The whole household had to function under a sort of quarantine of silence and any decisions demanding his attention simply had to wait for a spell of idleness.

Offhand I am unable to name one writer of any consequence who was not known as an ogre during periods of creation even though the product of his agonizing might be a delightful or amusing thing to titillate the public. My father's stories may have made anonymous millions chuckle, but he was no laughing matter grinding and groaning them out. For writing is one of the toughest ways of making a living and the most unpredictable.

Writing as a profession looks so easy. It appears that all one requires are a typewriter and paper. Easy?

My father wrote me: "When I first started writing I reckon I got more refusals than anyone that ever lived. I had one yarn turned down thirty-five times, then sent it to a big league magazine that I had never before thought of approaching and connected. . . ."

It wasn't until I began in the writing field myself that I came to understand my father's moods which puzzled and offended me as a child. He was likely to be gruff or rude if caught with his thought in the middle of a plot. Or he might just be absent-minded and vague. There was no telling without trying him.

Few adults can understand the mechanics of a writer's mind weaving the line of a yarn and it is impossible to explain to a child demanding affection by way of attention. Just as an adult is offended and rejected by rude handling, so is a child who is a person in its own right—if only a small person.

Thus my father estranged me, from a time long before memory begins. He didn't mean to, of course, and never understood why his child was (in my sister's words) "nasty to him." A small child functions on the theory of tit-for-tat. He was rude to me; ergo, I was rude right back. He rejected me (so I thought) ; ergo, vice versa.

My father once entered the plea, through a column, that he was not a natural born parent. He seemed to think that explained all and allowed him to bow gracefully out of parental duties. I never did and do not now accept such a plea.

It is palatable nonsense to argue that some people are natural born parents and some not. All of us run into knots and bolts in our struggles to raise little people without boggling the job. None escapes mistakes. I have seen child psychologists waving the white flag at their own efforts.

The point that escaped my father, among millions of others like him, was that children demand attention—it's their security—and if they don't get it they won't give it.

I never went home again nor did I write to my father until the last days. We were cordial when we'd meet, and at times there was almost a sense of closeness, but inwardly I still was burned up with resentment over fancied wrongs, and ready to explode whenever anyone asked that old question about father's footsteps. Even special holidays passed without communication between us until the last Christmas, 1945.

My dear Son:

Your letter was my finest holiday gift. It made Christmas a most wonderful event for me, indeed. Thanks, too, for your telegram which arrived Christmas morning. . . .

I am glad you and Mary both enjoyed Christmas. It was always a tremendous day in our family.

As children you used to receive the most fabulous gifts from the people of the world of sport. I doubt that any youngsters in our walk of life ever had more. Maybe you had too much.

I remember returning from Paris once with a load of gifts for Mary that cost Nell Henry, the wife of Milt Henry, a once famous jockey, and the proprietress of the world-renowned New York Bar, over a thousand dollars. An ermine coat was among them. The novelty of receiving became an old story to you both. Even after you were pretty well grown, as you will remember, I made quite an occasion of Christmas.

My apartment is decorated with wreaths and holly and tiny Christmas trees and looks very gay, though there is no one here but me to enjoy it.

I got a raft of stuff in the way of perishables that

I am disposing of among my friends because I can't very well use it. . . .

Take care of yourself, son.

Affectionately,
Dad

P.S. Your Cincinnati's A.A. seems to be doing a marvelous job judging from what you tell me about the party for the kids. HAPPY NEW YEAR

Our Christmas and birthday gifts were fabulous for as long as I can remember. These presents spoiled us only in the sense that they left us little to want. I mean they did not spoil us by making us recalcitrant or any harder on the furniture than we already were.

Many of these fabulous gifts actually were overwhelming to a small child and sometimes were downright frightening. They always were more than I wanted or could handle.

One Christmas midnight, the hour we children were awakened after Santa Claus had taken his departure, presumably through the dumbwaiter hatch of the apartment building, my sleepy eyes fell on a huge electric train my father had assembled. The train was almost big enough to ride and I was afraid to go near it.

Another Christmas my father presented me with a valuable scale model motorboat that went so fast it would have ripped right out of Central Park's lagoon where little people sail their small craft. For a birthday he gave me a scale model sailboat with a mainmast five feet tall. I couldn't even lift the thing.

Again, he once asked me what I wanted for Christmas. I mentioned a motion picture projector and cited the model I had in mind, a cheap, child's gimmick cranked by hand. He turned up with an electric sixteen-millimeter job.

In each case I was stunned by the immensity of the gifts and appalled by the prospect of mastering them without winding up with a pile of junk that would bring down the hairbrush. My father took my silence for disapproval or disappointment and plainly felt I was an ungrateful urchin. In turn, I felt the expenditure was a heavy-handed attempt to buy me in some way.

Many a rich kid no doubt has had the same experience and the poor kid may be better off, even if he doesn't realize it, with his ten-penny toy, provided he has parents with a wealth of good feeling. I leave this to the child experts to pass on.

There never was anything my father could have bought that would have pleased me more than some parental approval which could have been expressed without cost or, at most, through some gismo with no more than sentimental value. It apparently didn't occur to my father until his last days, when he was alone with so little time, that any importance could be attached to such gifts. He made this plain with his gifts of that last Christmas.

A Runyon family crest which he sent in the form of a hard wax impression was copied from a column of family histories in the *Cincinnati Enquirer* years ago. It carried the story of the Runions of France who settled in New Jersey and then spread through this republic. The name became Runyan and that was the original spelling of our name.

My father's father changed the name to Runyon in his days as a wandering newspaperman because that's the way printers were always spelling it anyway. Ironically, when printers of today botch the copy they spell it Runyan.

Before the family history came to hand I once asked my father about our ancestors. Said he, "We come from a long line of Huguenot horse thieves who were run out of France by posses." It was his way of dismissing pretensions about family. He took people the way they are, not as their ancestors were. He repeated his view on family front in his note accompanying his last Christmas gifts.

Dear Damon:

The frivolous-looking money clip enclosed was given me by Mike Todd, producer of a show called *Star and Garter* as a souvenir of that opus a couple of years ago and I pass it on to you as a keepsake of no great intrinsic value that has its uses at times.

The seal enclosed belongs to Mary. It is the Runyon family crest and she has always treasured it. I think you both once had rings that bore the crest, but they have probably disappeared as such things do.

You might want to replace them some day or otherwise use the crest, though personally I have never placed much store, as the saying is, on those things.

The cuffs are a slight variation from the usual. The belt and pencil are just by way of addenda. I just got the little notebook as a souvenir from Major

Bowes. Give it to Mary. I hope you like the mufflers and ties, and with all good wishes for a nice Christmas and a Happy New Year, I am

Affectionately,
Dad

I'm afraid all my sympathy that Christmas didn't go out to my father. For he had been the dominant force in setting the course that brought us to this day. And my sister, that gentle little girl of yesteryear who'd sought only affection and attention, was spending that Christmas in a private hospital for the mentally ill as a consequence of that nervous breakdown previously mentioned.

5

The Runyon guys and dolls tales of Broadway, I believe, will gain more respect with time, and some day may be foisted on students as homework for study in English IV, for in them the short story form was brought to perfection.

There is some argument as to who invented the short story with the neat plot and twist ending. Some will go back to de Maupassant, or Aesop, while others plug Poe and still others will swear by O. Henry. No matter who started the form, I think careful study will show the doctors of learning that in the Runyon stories the form was rounded out to where nothing could be added nor removed. Since so few writers could match the standard of this type it was dropped almost universally.

I am not beating any drum but pointing out something that, as far as I know, has escaped the high minds of literature. It is possible the time-pent "guys and dolls" of the Prohibition era led the professors to overlook the perfection of the frame in which the characters cavorted. I leave the rest to writers of dust-catchers to explore. I add only a few points of light where I can.

A controversy grew over whether Runyon characters were fictional or had real counterparts. Columnists Louis Sobol and Dorothy Kilgallen of the *New York Journal-American* argued they were fictions while columnist Walter Winchell of the *New York Mirror* and all the ships at sea took the opposite view to claim they were real. Well, to quote Professor H. L. Mencken, the eminent Baltimore boob-bumper, "you may be right."

Take "All Horse Players Die Broke." This short story involved a once successful handicapper, Unser Fritz, who lost even his title to the rank of handicapper and "is spoken of as a bum." The story opens with the tale teller (always unidentified) standing under the elms in front of the Grand Union Hotel in Saratoga when who comes along but Unser Fritz.

This actually happened, give or take a few details. We were walking under the elms along Broadway in Saratoga when who comes along but—I spare his name, for he was indeed real. He was in fact a once wealthy handicapper who had become a bum. He was "maybe seventy-five," greasy, and threw a scent three yards. We stood to windward while my father pressed him with questions and scribbled notes.

Standing there he told his story in low tone and with such a thick German accent we had difficulty with his text. The rough essentials are in the story, even to a doll he showered with jewels until she held her chin so high she wouldn't ride in the same elevator with him "because I am not always tidy enough to suit her." The fictional doll is named Emerald Em, but I understood the real doll was the original Diamond Lil.

From these essentials of Unser Fritz' real story my father built up a 5,000-word fictional yarn. The rest is a hodgepodge of fact and fancy and not all of it is from Unser Fritz' real story. The thing that puzzled me at the time was why my father suddenly picked that evening in Saratoga to get this character's story question-answer style. For Unser Fritz had been around for years that I knew of.

He was one of the baggy beggars who slipped from the shadowy shores along Broadway to waylay my father in midstream of the crowd. He followed from track to track the horses that broke him. He traveled by sleeping in the railroad horsecars. My father long ago had sketched him for me and, as in the fictional story, Unser Fritz "seldom comes right out and asks anybody for anything unless things are very desperate with him, indeed."

My father always slipped Unser Fritz exactly two dollars. That was the old fellow's standing bet. If he got one dollar he would hold it until he could corner another. He always was hoping to hit the comeback trail even though by the time I knew him he was tottering with age. It was my impression that it was from him that my father got the expression, "All horse players die broke."

When I say my father slipped him the money I mean slipped. He always pumped the hand of this flotsam so the bobs would pass unseen. Behind the grime and grease of this ancient my father recognized a fellow human being still fanning a spark of dignity.

Why did he single out that one evening in Saratoga to get the details of Unser Fritz' story? He always kept filed in his mind the possibility that such a character would make a story. That night he just felt in the mood "to work," or had no better idea on file, or was loser on the season and needed to write something to get even.

He had laid the meeting ground by years of shaking a greasy hand in Broadway's glare of lights and looks. He could not have gotten the story the first time around. He did not slip the singles with any repayment in mind, however. It just so happened that in Unser Fritz' case kindness paid off thousandsfold.

In all the Runyon stories the same background could be noted about the characters. In "The Brain Goes Home," about a big gambler with an accumulation of dolls around and about who bar their doors when he shows up well-stabbed, anyone who knew the Prohibition era will recognize Arnold Rothstein, a fellow customer at Lindy's restaurant.

But Rothstein gets shot, not stabbed, and he does not stagger around to a lot of dolls' houses, but comes out of a hotel service entrance to the street and is rushed to Polyclinic Hospital where he dies neat in a surgical bed. The Brain may resemble Rothstein but what happens to him is strictly Runyon.

In "Romance in the Roaring Forties" it would not be hard to pin down the original inspiration for Waldo Winchester of *The Morning Item* who "writes about the goings-on in night clubs, such as fights, and one thing or another, and also about who is running around with who, including guys and dolls." But I leave it to a realist like Walter Winchell to say whether what happens to the character is true.

Another controversy stewed over whether the real Broadwayites talk in the present tense slanguage used by the fictional Runyon guys and dolls. The controversy was taken seriously in England where the Runyon stories were as popular as they were here. Do guys and dolls really talk like that?

Unser Fritz' English was mangled like a shirt in a same-day laundry, yet in "All Horse Players Die Broke" he speaks pure Broadwayese, or more correctly, Runyonese. What escapes most who claim Runyon reported what he had heard is that in his stories an anonymous "I" tells the tales. It is he who speaks in the present tense even when he is quoting someone like Unser Fritz. The anonymous "I," of course, is Runyon.

It is true that some Broadwayites, especially in the Lindy's set, fall into the present tense in their gabble. Gambler Frank Costello had the Senate Crime Committee Senators feeling they'd hit on something big when he said "I have" slot machines in Louisiana until an hour of questioning and explanation finally made clear that what he meant was "I *had*" the one-armed bandits, but not at present.

However, even those to whom the present tense comes naturally usually mix in the past tense, too. In the Runyon stories this present tense was pure, carried out to every word, and it was laborious writing to make it read smoothly. If anyone talks like that along the Big Street they come after the fact, or rather fiction.

Many of the characters in the Runyon stories were built up and embellished small shots, race track touts and others of more dubious occupations, mostly harmless and no bargain in the flesh. A few were patterned after heavies of more dangerous fame.

My father did not approve of law-breaking despite the whimsical viewpoint in his stories but he was a western realist. In theory the republic was against dice and drink, but in fact was shaking both behind the door. The gambler and gangster were merchants who supplied the demand.

Most gangsters I met had a drive for respectability, dressed like Wall Street brokers, and spoke softly and politely even if they murdered the king's English as easily as enemies. Their booze may have been poison to some citizens, but otherwise they did not go out of their way to shorten the insurance odds on anyone outside their own circle.

My father could understand this setup because it was not a far cry from the Old West where every citizen packed the law on his hip. In both cases it wasn't until some innocent bystanders got pegged accidentally by stray or wild shots that the pious set up a hue and cry for legit law to cage the careless cutups.

His column, like the short stories, usually was peopled by the uncommon characters of sports and Broadway or dealt with their ideas. He once tried the heavy think routine but gave it up to entertain the readers. "The Brighter Side," as the column finally was called, was more a stage than a platform. He went from sports to this editorial page feature in 1937 and it always was a syndicated success, but the biggest jump in interest came when he was dying on his feet.

September 6, 1946

My dear Son:

. . . Not much to report here, except of a sudden my column took fire with the boss people, including Mr. Hearst, and he is prodding the editors to be sure and get it in the papers, which only makes it necessary for me to keep on a regular schedule instead of doing it when I felt like it.

Newspaper work is, of course, not of great importance to me now and sometimes I wonder why I keep at it. I am commencing to think it is force of habit. . . .

My plans for the immediate future are not settled but I am getting restless and will probably go somewhere, I don't know where. Take care of yourself.

Affectionately,
Dad

My father's column took fire because he had turned to reporting about plain people, what happened to them and their reactions, the joys and sorrows usually ignored by newspapers. A minor tenement fire considered too small to rate space in the big city papers, yet a shattering calamity to those who experienced it. A street fight which even police didn't notice but which packed all the same essential human actions and reactions of a war.

My father began spreading these daily dramas when he took to riding around the city at night with Walter Winchell responding to police alarms over the prowl car radio system. They made a perfect team, my father noted, since Winchell liked to talk and he liked to listen. For my father it was a means of fighting loneliness and an excuse to keep from going home with his constant companion, Death.

In a sense it was a turning back. He began to cover the big city like a small town, where he had started out, where every little event is big. He may have gotten the idea from my experience in Cincinnati where I was going the route the other way. I had started out in the big city and was discovering the importance of the human events considered unimportant by most editors. I had been writing him and sending clips about this approach.

"For the first time," I wrote my father, "I am entering into a newspaper gag which would indicate that I apparently have lost all reason. This week (Sept. 9, 1946) I am to be 'Mr. Ace' in a piece of foolishness which has an obvious tie-up with the forthcoming George Raft picture of that name. . . . I am to appear in certain parts of downtown Cincinnati at specified times with $100 cash to give the first person who identifies me through pictures in *The Post* that you, my father, wouldn't recognize. . . ."

My dear Son:

Thanks for your letter. Thanks, too, for your kind words about my columns. I hope your cold has cleared up. No one in this world ever got knocked out by a cold the way I used to, though since my operation any I may have had have been slight, and I take no precautions against them whatever.

Previously I was a nut on drafts, exposures, etc., went overshoed and overcoated and often medicined for colds . . . so when I got it, I wouldn't have it.

Don't tell me that old stunt you speak of is still alive! I was the man with the money in Denver nigh onto forty years ago, come next grass, only it was not $100, as I remember. It was $25. And I don't want to brag but I was the greatest newspaper stunt man of my time, not only in executing stunts but devising them.

I used to travel all over Colorado with a sketch artist named Finch doing a feature called "Me and Mr. Finch," covering fairs and festivals and church sociables and everything that brought as many as forty persons together anywhere. I did the writing and Finch the illustrating, but on the side Finch would give public chalk talks and I would lecture.

It was a stunt in which Finch as "Doc Bird" (his cartoon character) met me as Santa Claus, at the Union Depot in Denver one Christmas week with a band and attended by a zillion children, that caused the *Post* to hire us away from the *News*.

I put on scores of different stunts for the *Post*, including a race against a mythical world record on home bicycle trainers staged on a platform in front of the *Post* building. I think our new record still stands in the book.

I refereed prize fights, a practice that Gene Fowler, who was more or less my successor, continued. I went up in a balloon. I slept in flophouses as a hobo for color for a story. I did a hundred and one similar stunts and had a lot of fun doing them. I did not follow up my stunt career in New York to any great extent, but devised promotions like the Milk Fund fights that produced a couple of million dollars.

I always made covering a standard story like a big race or a ball game more or less of a stunt. At one Futurity I covered it up at the starting gate, or rather at the barrier, as there were no gates in those days, standing at the side of old Mars Cassidy, the starter. When the great Pittsburgh slugger Honus Wagner came to town I covered the game, not from the press box, but from the bleachers and a rear view of Honus.

When the great Bill Phelon came in with the Cincinnati Reds and a live squirrel in his pocket, I sat alongside him in the press box and wrote my whole story around the reactions of the squirrel. Of course the game itself was an unimportant routine transaction late in the season. I always considered stunts more or less reportorial relaxation and I think I would go out today if they asked me and be (the name has just come to me—I mean of that Denver experience) "The Mysterious Mr. Baffle," just for fun.

Pardon an old gentleman's mumbling.

Dad

My father once admitted he would abandon his belief that the "measure of success is money" as soon as "the world arranges a system of compensation in luxury for an artistic failure equal to that which derives from a commercial success." Meanwhile, he wrote, "an old rule with me is never decry a success."

On my first visit with my father after I'd left home and school to go to work I sounded off at great length with sharp criticism of a certain widely syndicated columnist. I then was a "pony" editor, or one jump ahead of office boy, in the Cleveland bureau of United Press at a salary of $25 a week. My father listened patiently while I ran off at the mouth. Then when I paused for breath he said very casual-like, "That fellow you are knocking makes $250,000 a year. How much do you make?"

On our last visit together, when we were discussing various problems he was about to leave, he fell gloomy talking about my sister's illness involving great distress to us both and high expense. Fumbling for something comforting to say, I pointed out that at least finances weren't a problem in the Runyon case. "After all," I observed, "you make a lot of money. . . ." He broke in with a wave of his hand. "Yes," the voiceless one wrote, "but I spend a lot." He grinned.

Indeed he did. Money itself meant nothing to him. The mere possession of the long green gave him no feeling of security. He had to spend to get the feel of the power of a bank account. He liked to swagger (self-consciously) into Sulka's and flip off an order for a dozen $15 to $25 ties, to travel in a drawing room, to live when away in a hotel suite, to dine at the Colony. Money also allowed him to indulge certain kindnesses.

He was an easy touch for the more bedraggled

touchers along Broadway. When he pushed along with the crowd that flows like a two-current river on the Great White Way at night he was a mark for a standing army of baggy beggars, some of them uncommon characters fallen on evil days, who would shoot out of the shadows to sidle up to him in the mainstream. Some didn't have to ask. He refused none.

This form of charity sometimes seemed quixotic, since nine times out of ten the handout went to booze or bangtails. My father knew this, but he had a theory. He pointed out that there was no way of knowing when the tenth case might come along where the touch would do some good. He remembered his own hard times.

The haunting memory of hungry times was what kept him doing work he didn't particularly care for, even when he could have moved on to other fields.

Dear Son:

I feel pretty good now. Looks as if I'll have to dig up a new line as all the boys are starting to imitate the Runyon-Winchell pilgrimages. I mean in the character of the stuff. If the others like it, it must be all right. Let me tell you a secret. I never liked doing a column until lately. I could always make so much more money with much less effort on fiction. But lately for some reason I have taken a fancy to columning, trying to prove, I think, a theory that people are more interested in people and in things that happen to people than in politics. I would be willing to make a bet that a guy who stays sober and works as hard as you are working and doing the kind of working you are doing is bound to get somewhere in time. . . .

My father never liked writing a column for the simple reason that he could not say what he wanted to say. Even columnists have reins on them. My father was supposed to stick to "The Brighter Side" and the most optimistic would admit that was a strict limitation especially in wartime.

He was forced to devise gimmicks for the rare occasions when he wanted to sneak over the limits. One of these was to make it appear he wasn't responsible for what he wrote, as in the columns featuring "My Old Man," whose views were cynical, caustic and cutting. I have seen these picked up and used literally as "quotes" from my father's father, my grandfather, but of course they were from my old man.

My father suppressed himself and ground out "The Brighter Side" even when life was darkest, as when Death came calling, because somewhere along the line he had come to the choice all writers face— whether to work for love or money. He wrote what he wrote because that was what he got paid the most for, not because it was what he wanted to say.

He was, as he himself put it, a "hired Hessian."

My Dear Son:
I haven't been any too well lately and this is just a note to let you know I haven't forgotten you. I have not been able to write my column for a couple

of weeks but managed to knock off a few the last three days . . .

I am up and around but inordinately tired all the time. I have never been able to break myself of the habit of staying up late and sleeping most of the day. I have an assignment from *Cosmopolitan* to do a three-installment story that I have not been able to start on through lack of energy. But I am hoping to return to form pretty soon.

I was deeply interested in your last letter. I am so glad that the problems of others now concern you even more than your own. You were inclined to be a little self-centered, a fault of many of us. I was the same way a long time. Now I believe if I am remembered for anything it will be for what I did or tried to do for others.

And speaking of your thoughts about the Church, I will be most happy if ever you return to it. I know of no greater solace to the human mind and soul than religion. I think I would have made an excellent priest or minister of the gospel. I have always had a bent toward religion.

I think my greatest misfortune was in getting caught in a current that demanded a certain standard of living and it took money to meet that standard.

I would have been better off if I had remained a struggling and obscure fellow of no great means in a small community where I might have found peace and contentment in plain living and spiritual considerations instead of becoming a big town by-line writer always fighting to keep up there and to make money.

" 'And what good came of it at last,' quoth Little Peterkin."

But give my love to Mary and keep plenty for yourself.

In Affection,
Dad

6

My religious trend of that day was a passing thing and my father's remarks on his own attitude—that he would have made "an excellent priest or minister" —were the expression of a dying man. For he would have no more made a priest or minister than I would. Both of us were reared freethinkers from the crib and the frock would have choked us. Our bent for freedom, however, often brought us into conflict with those around us.

My dear Son:

Thanks for your letter. You certainly have plenty on your hands and mind. I will be delighted to see you when you come east, and perhaps I can ease some of your problems. I have no fear whatever of your drinking. I do not think you will ever drink again. I do not believe you are that big a chump after what you have been through and what you know now. . . .

The most disquieting note in your letter was your suggestion that you are not happy in your office.

You are probably like I was—pretty self-assured and independent, but I learned to give and take. If I lost my temper, which was not infrequent, I learned to apologize.

Consideration for the rights of one's fellow worker is a great thing. I used to flatter myself that I was pretty popular in newspaper offices because I was always a willing and agreeable worker even when they were peering over my shoulder on a deadline which you say irks you. I thought it rather flattering.

And let me tell you something. You can always learn a little from another guy in the newspaper business even if you don't think he knows as much as you do.

I liked the yarn you enclosed. You have it in you to make a great newspaperman, as I have told you before.

Probably I forgot to tell you that part of newspaper greatness is getting along in and with an office. You would be surprised how much of my reputation came from the mob inside being always eager to give me the best of it. . . .

But watch your health. You are not hereditarily strong. You used to smoke a great deal and I presume you still do and I think I ought to tell you that I believe my present difficulty may trace to the inordinate amount of smoking I did all my life. This is not a lecture, just a hint . . .

I am glad you are studying scriptwriting technique on your own hook. A man who can turn out

movie scripts can get rich especially if they are
original. Stick to that study above all things, because
if you have a good notion of how to construct a script
you need never worry about a job. . . .

Dad

My last visit with my father was the idea of Cincinnati friends and colleagues of the fourth estate.
The project took little urging and a small collection.
The *Post* granted me leave without any hemming
and hawing, for the editor, Carl D. Groat, was a contemporary of my father. Clutching my borrowed
satchel and stake in a death grip against slickers,
I was off to the big city to settle old scores.

My father was out when I arrived past midnight
feeling like a rube in the plush Buckingham. He'd
posted notes around on various doors to guide me in
his suite and one suggested that I should hit the hay
if I was weary as he would not be back soon. Next
thing I knew he was shaking me awake past noon,
grinning and thrusting a note under my nose for my
nearsighted squint: "Breakfast is ready."

When I staggered out, bleary-eyed, he was putting
the last of the dishes on the table in the living room,
so I pitched into a conglomeration of eggs and
salami, a favorite dish of his. When he settled opposite and fell to, I was struck by the fact that he was
bloated. I couldn't help comment, "Why, you're fat
as a pig!" He grinned and nodded vigorously as he
scribbled a note announcing he'd swollen to 195
pounds.

My sister already had reported on the little tricks
one had to learn living with a man who'd once com-

manded all the conversation but who now was mute. It was a new experience for me to pump the gas since previously I always was on the mute side when my father was around.

It was uncomfortable and tedious business until one became acclimated. Talking by scribbled notes obviously was tiresome, so the idea was to save him the effort, to keep conversation one-sided. Questions, for example, were best phrased so he could reply with a nod or shake of his head.

He also had a repertory of grimaces and gestures which served after a fashion once one had become accustomed to being around him. And, when he felt one had become used to his affliction, he would shyly try a whisper or two. People similarly stricken mute can learn to talk—there are at least two methods— but my father didn't try. He felt there wasn't enough time to make it worth the effort.

My first struggle to lead the conversation floundered from one inane subject to another as I felt my way along. It was difficult to tell whether he was interested. Indeed, that was true even when he could talk. I knew him to be a man of such moods that frequently he'd just as soon everyone shut up, and my awareness of this proved a stumbling handicap. In the course of my babbling I commented that the breakfast was excellent. He flushed and grinned.

"I cooked it myself," he scribbled.

I was first amazed, then moved by this announcement. Here was a man who could, and always would, demand room service instanter, and it had better be the best. He didn't have to lift a finger if he didn't want to—and he usually didn't. Yet for this occasion he'd personally dished up a spread and he was blushing pleased that I liked it. The gesture made me feel closer than ever before to my father.

His communication of affection usually was through such gestures. He never made a display as did my mother, who was more likely to cry hosannah and hallelujah, fling her arms around our necks, laugh and wrinkle our clothes with tears after an absence, such as an afternoon in the park. My father often appeared a cold cookie, but he was just shy at making a show of feeling, except perhaps for anger.

I found he had completely reorganized his routine, habits and attitudes since Death had come to live with him, and there were corresponding difficulties in adjustment for anyone who'd been around in his rigid regime of past years.

He no longer held to a schedule of rising and sleeping, but did as the spirit moved him. When he wearied he went to bed. When he found himself punching the pillow, and thoughts of doom loomed too large, he got up, dressed quickly and went out, no matter the hour. Dying, he lived wiser than when living. Since life was placed under limit he came to fill each waking minute.

The first day I visited he went to bed and I sought out a local A.A. chapter in a former church building, still gaseous from the sweat of the faithful, and in this depressing atmosphere I spent the time with an imbecile who confessed he "wasn't quite dry yet" but was playing the sneak on himself by nipping beer. My prescription was for him to quit on the spot or take the address of the nearest booze emporium.

After laboring in the vineyard I returned to dress for dinner, meaning I took a shower and put on a different tie, as I had only one presentable suit since my struggles in reformation.

One of my father's friends came into the room and inspected me. He demanded to know if that was the "best suit you have." He also objected to a red tie I'd fancied. At first all my old feelings of inadequacy welled up. I started to stammer some lame excuse when my new-found self came to the front and told the character to mind his own business.

We proceeded to Lindy's, as usual, where my father stuffed, and thence to Madison Square Garden a block away to watch Neanderthals belabor each other. There was a mix-up in tickets and my father was barred at the door to this palace he'd been instrumental in promoting. He stood silent and unprotesting, jostled unnoticed by the passing mob, until some hierarchy was reached and the gate was opened to him. He looked somehow lonely and pathetic as he waited patiently for the jakes on the door to have done with this tomfoolery.

Afterward we went across the street to the Carnival, one of those dim-lit smoke-filled rooms jokers call night clubs, where we watched Milton Berle cavort and sweat through pre-television routines. I caught my father sneaking peeks past my shoulder at a pretty little doll who couldn't have been over eighteen under layers of make-up. Worse, I caught her sneaking peeks at him.

"You're not doing bad for a guy your age," I commented. He gave his shy grin and scribbled, "She likes me."

We adjourned to Lindy's where the usual parade

of characters passed, although I noted that they didn't try to stay as long as they once did. Berle came in and collapsed in a chair, announcing the obvious, that he was exhausted from two hours on stage in every act. My father took him to task for using "blue" material, arguing that the clown prince didn't need to stoop for laughs.

Berle also suddenly was dead serious although he usually is "on stage" all the time. In his case I don't know whether it was due to being in the company of a dying man or because he was just plain weary. But I was beginning to notice the habit of people going straight-faced around my father. I finally went off to bed, being accustomed to hours of a day laborer, while he played gin rummy the night through with friends in the Buckingham.

Next noon he routed me out again with a note saying, "Call room service and order breakfast." He listed what he wanted. Room service was not serving breakfast at that hour. I relayed this information with some misgivings, expecting my father to wax indignant over such lack of accommodation. To my surprise he simply shrugged. He beckoned me to a window and pointed to a cafeteria across the street. "Go get yourself some breakfast," he wrote.

"What about you?" I asked. He shrugged again. "I'll get a glass of milk from the icebox," he wrote. I was astounded by this new order of things. Once upon a time he would have raged that there was a conspiracy against him if an egg showed up at the table overdone by half a minute. Now he was shrugging off not only the lack of service but the whole works.

It seems that circumstances had forced my father

to reorganize his way of living to a way of dying. The sad part was that he and everyone around him would have been happier if he'd done it years sooner. His old habits were a trial to many. I found him an enjoyable change from his former persnickity character. Neither my sister nor I found it at all unpleasant to be with this dying man, although some of those around him complained he presented difficulties, even to being depressing. The whole time I was with him neither his ailment nor death were even mentioned.

But then I was trained never to notice openly any physical defects in another person. I could talk to a person with half a face and never let on I noticed anything unusual. In fact I have talked with a lot of two-faced people without letting on I was wise. This training comes in handy to a reporter, but it can be annoying to others since by the same token I am not likely to hand out any compliments.

I got that way because of the dark secret which never was discussed in our family. Even my father had never mentioned it to me although he knew how I felt. I wanted to resolve this while there yet was time. I didn't want that unspoken bitterness to stand forever. But how to bring it up?

His condition, forcing him to breathe through the metal tube in his throat, was such that undue emotional disturbance might set him to choking to death on the spot. I pondered whether to risk demanding his answer to the void between us—about my mother. What had happened to bring us all to this day?

My father and I were talking one night in his hotel suite when he wearied of using the typewriter as his "voice" and moved to an easy chair. As he wrote on pads for the purpose, with printed heads reading "Damon Runyon Says," I stood at his side so I could read his "conversation."

All of a sudden he wrote, "Why did your mother drink?"

After showing it to me he sat staring straight ahead waiting for an answer. It was slow in coming since I was caught completely off-guard. It wasn't lack of an answer that stumped me. I knew through my own experience battling the booze, and I knew he must know by the same token.

Alcoholism, like other human aches and ailments, is at once a mental and physical problem. There is no cure for the rumpot. His case can only be arrested. As for what causes alcoholism, theories abound for the choosing. The fact is that no one knows the exact answers.

I speak as the A.A.'s act, only from experience, both my own and that of alcoholic colleagues I have encountered in my travels through strife.

People like the Runyons just weren't built for boozing in the first place. Then came the emotional crags. In my mother's case these included the myriad frustrations and no doubt resentment against my father's success as well as the other dolls he chased.

I realized that the way my father put his question was a blind. What he meant was, "Do you still blame me?"

I would have liked to question him about the way he felt about a lot of things that had happened to us all, but I didn't. Because as he sat there dying by inches, breathing through a metal tube in his throat and in silent pain, I felt that here was a very courageous man, a fellow with heart, filled with weaknesses, but filled, too, with great strengths which made him own up and brace himself to face the truth though the effort was pushing his luck. And he was thinking of his fellow man in sorrow which he might relieve even at great cost to himself.

He was making one of his odd acts of affection, for he knew the subject meant so much to me, and the gentle way he faced up to it was as fine and tender a gesture as any flinging of the arms or splendid speeches. He didn't go into a lot of who-struck-John. He didn't tell me. He asked me. I fumbled an answer something like this:

I thought my mother's leaning on liquor was the result of a lot of factors—her childhood, her inability to face facts, the circumstances of the time, some of the crowd she fell in with, her physical make-up. She just wasn't gaited right. It was not anyone else's fault and once she got started there was nothing anyone could do except herself. And she didn't want to save herself.

I didn't go into the fact that I had come at long last to realize through my own battle with the bottle that the only thing he could have done under the circumstances was just what he did—walk out. He couldn't save her or himself by staying. He, too, would have been doomed, and he had to save himself. For no one else will save us except ourself. What he had done had not doomed her. She doomed herself.

He sat silent for a moment. Then he gestured with hands outward and palms up, meaning "That's that."

When the time came for me to leave my father for the last time—on his feet, that is—I found he'd gone to bed although it was the shank of the afternoon. Though that wasn't out of kilter with his new habits, I sensed when I peeked into his bedroom that he wasn't asleep. He just didn't want to say good-by.

As I was about to go out the door the phone rang and I had to rouse him. I carried on the conversation for him and then came the moment he had tried to avoid. I knew how it was with him, because it was the same with me, so I didn't make a production of it.

"So long, Dad," I said.

His lips formed the words, "So long, Son."

He broke just a little—he put his arm around my shoulder and squeezed.

7

Now in the deepening twilight of my father's life I sought to close the remaining gaps between us without, as usual, retreating in fear and confusion if he turned testy.

This would be a tight trick because I determined for once to oppose him when I felt in the right even at the risk of undoing previous patching. In view of his condition it had to be a closely calculated risk.

With a well-ordered revolt I could rise from under his domination to become a free personality in my own right; for him a jot of humility could turn into a tower of strength. At least he would have something to think about.

The fear of him was still within. Always there was the weakening dread of the all-powerful giant, the great god Father, who could crush a child with a glare, whose word could cast out; the presence that demanded love but drew fear.

When we were very small a big event in our lives

was the coming of the comics each Sunday morning. Our father would bring the Sunday newspapers home with him at three o'clock in the morning, read in bed, and invariably fall asleep with the papers scattered over and around him.

He never put "the funnies," as we called them, outside of his room for us. We never could contain ourselves from the early morning rising hours of little people until noon when he would be awakening. So my sister and I would venture into his room after them.

We went about the project like two small mice sneaking cheese from under the nose of a snoozing tomcat. First there was the opening of his bedroom door, inch by inch, sucking in our breaths with every slight squeak of the hinges.

Then tippy-toe to his bedside. There was much nervous giggling and elbowing each other for quiet as we approached the sleeping giant. He slept like an idling donkey engine, so we could gauge our progress by the decibels of the snoring.

If he'd suddenly snort and fall silent we'd hold our breaths and stand stock still until the breathing of the sleeping would signal a go-ahead. Then we'd proceed to a point where we could lay hands on the papers. Sometimes this called for a tittering estimate of the situation.

Invariably the vital papers would be pinioned by an elbow, or a leg flung willy-nilly, or—disaster— by the great torso itself. The more courageous one of the moment would seize a corner of the "funnies" and test with a tug.

Sometimes luck was with us and the gentle move

would be just enough to disturb the giant into rolling over, freeing the prize. Mostly it seemed that fate was against us and we had to labor long to ease the papers out without waking him.

If our efforts produced the first vague mumblings of consciousness our hearts would be caught up with terror. At times we induced a faint fluttering of the eyelids. A few expeditions provoked total recognition which sent us in hasty retreat full of fear and confusion.

The awakened giant would smile softly or at worst mutter sleepily, then turn over and sleep on.

We'd seize the "funnies" boldly and tumble tinkling with triumph into the living room to spread the sheets over the floor where we could sprawl in comfort, feeling big again. We were glowing secure with our prize, our victory, our "funnies."

But of course the gaudy sheets were only the evidence in hand of victory. The real triumph was felt. We had revolted against the taboos of the castle; we had defied the giant in his lair; we had risked the peace, the status quo, our security; and we had won.

We lost bigger ventures.

We'd again retreat in fear and confusion, but now frequently falling over ourselves.

My sister idolized our father and sought to hold to the little touches of affection she'd known those first four years of tenderness. I talked of revolt—a break for freedom—and sought her alliance, but she remained passively devoted.

I went on lashing out wildly through life until I collapsed in drink, defeated by fear, confusion—and myself. Now that I was attaining some sensible command of myself I knew I had to conquer that gnawing terror while there yet was time. And there wasn't much time.

The first major test came when I asked a friend, a newspaperwoman, to give my father a personal message when she went to New York from Cincinnati. She was insulted by self-appointed friends of his who posted themselves as guards around him.

I'd suffered this kind of indignity before in silence but now I gave him a discrete whiff of grapeshot.

Dear Damon:

. . . . Your letter seems to indicate that you have a problem of some kind. If it has to do with money let me know and I will help you.

. . . . [My divorce] cleaned me out pretty well but all I need to make money is a little health and time and a typewriter and given those I will be back fast. I don't waste time contemplating my sad estate and never did.

Y met Miss X [1] through some friend of his who is a friend of hers. I was not feeling well that day and in fact went home and went to bed the day he met her. I do not know what he told her but I do know that there were reasons why I could not see anyone at that particular time, much less a lady who was a stranger to me.

I have a full appreciation of Miss X's position and I am most certainly deeply grateful to her for her kindness to you and Mary. I am sorry that anything happened to give offense to her but it was without my knowledge and of course without my sanction

[1] Names are omitted for obvious reasons.

and I wish you would offer my personal apologies to her.

I saw F——— tonight. He said you didn't answer a couple of letters sent to you by persons on the coast interested in your work. I suppose you had your reasons. I was supposed to report to the Fox lot August 1 but I have to stick around here awhile to pick up some loose ends of the divorce inasmuch as it involves a complete change in my setup. Even then I may finally decide not to go. It is too far from the doctor.

I notice you do a lot of thinking about yourself and your problems. Sometimes when you are in a mood for thought give one to your old man who in two years was stricken by the most terrible malady known to mankind and left voiceless with a death sentence hanging over his head, who had a big career stopped cold, and had his domestic life shattered by divorce and his savings largely dissipated through the combination of evil circumstances.

All this at sixty-five years of age when most men's activity is completely ended.

Try that on your zither some day, my boy, especially when those low moods you mention strike you.

I have no one to help me in any way save when a good soul . . . drops around out of the goodness of his heart, no one to aid and comfort me. I have no permanent habitation, no possessions any more save a few clothes, and most of them were stolen the other day by a thief.

I repeat my offer: If money will help solve your problem, and I never knew many problems money wouldn't solve, let me know. You don't have to waste any thousand words to tell me how, as I am not apt to be interested in what for. I will endeavor to remember Mary's birthday but you better jog my memory if you think of it yourself.

I am glad you straightened Dr. Z out on my financial status. It is probably even worse than you implied despite the fact that I understand a radio announcer recently awarded me a visionally hundred thousand but I will manage to dig up enough to take care of your temporary disorder unless it is plumb over my head.

Meantime, you keep me in mind as an antidote to your own sad sad thoughts. . . .

In affection,
Dad

My father's divorce, obtained in Florida after a separation agreement gained by the second Mrs. Runyon, came as a surprise. After ending fourteen years of marriage to my father, on the eve of his death she married a young man. My father had gone through this Florida legal hurricane, in which he lost all the family property, without informing me.

Naturally this emotional upheaval, combined with the other distress he was suffering, had a lot to do with his whip-cracking retort. While I'd braced for a broadside my father's bitterness still stirred up all the old fear and confusion of yesteryear—fear of losing the fight to show myself independent of him, and confusion over whether to retreat or risk a stand. I took time to think over a reply.

My father in two thoughts expressed his basic

creed, which was Old American; one of them great and rapidly dying, the other fundamentally hollow but still going strong in this republic: 1. "All I need to make money is a little health and time and a typewriter," and 2. "I never knew many problems money wouldn't solve."

Give me a place to stand on and I can move the world. That idea lifted America to greatness and once was considered right smart. My father believed in and was made by the theory of freedom for the individual to use his own talents and be given room to forge as far as they would carry him.

His beliefs were based on the pragmatic test, does it work? This, too, was an essentially Old American philosophy rapidly falling into disuse. He believed in freedom for the individual simply because the idea worked better than any others which have been foisted on human beings since they first stood and contemplated the stars.

His circumstances, of course, were brought about largely by his own doing through that very freedom he stood for. There was nothing I could do or say there that could help; at most I could serve as a sounding board for him on which to vent his pent-up feelings.

His exaggerated bow to the power of money was typical and easily could have been shot full of holes, but I didn't try. It seemed to be one of the few measures of security he felt he could hold onto now that he believed he was alone.

Until he realized he wasn't alone, that he could turn in his last hours to someone he hadn't believed in, I would try taking a stand with even reason. All the time I had to keep in mind I was dealing unseen with a dying man.

I explained to my father it was not money but advice I sought as a writer. Money won't solve the problem of a writer with a knack but no outlet. Without a place to stand on, a writer not only can't move any worlds—he is rendered mute, like my mother who had something to say, a flair for saying it, but no place to speak.

It is like being in a bottle, beating on the side to attract notice, but no one will pull the cork.

This was a problem with which I was wrestling on *The Cincinnati Post* and the solution was of vital importance in the progress of my battle against booze. The writer also comes up against the question of whether he should keep plugging away at what he is doing or move on in hopes of a better outlet. This, of course, is true in almost any line of work.

I'd received an offer of a newspaper job in another city. Actually the foremost question at the time was how long my father had to live. I didn't want to make a major move only to be called away by death. The one way to find out was to ask him—and, of course, I couldn't do that.

I tried the trick of asking his advice. Perhaps he would tip his hand, all aces, all spades.

August 6, 1946

Dear Damon:

. . . I am not in a position to pass on your problem at the paper, and of course any change that you might deem fit to make would be approved by me or at least would not be disapproved if you think it would contribute to your happiness and well being. But I don't know what you call happiness on a newspaper.

I have worked over fifty years around newspapers and I never thought any of them knew what to do with their men, either, especially if they were not three-sheeting me and paying me a big salary.

I do not know your problems . . . but I do know it is a good thing I never permitted similar bedevilments to pull me down to a standstill. . . .

Stop squawking.

I return the letters from the coast. Answer them courteously and apologetically and say you have been sick or tied up or something and that you have not yet decided just what you are going to do but that you will not forget them.

I liked the little human interest clip.

In affection,
Dad

Looking back, older and wiser, it's easier to see the problem and the solution—and the fact that my father couldn't know either for all his more than fifty years in the newspaper mills. For we had faced different problems in different eras as different personalities and, like all parents and children, we were a generation apart.

The real problem was that we didn't realize that.

My father set out barefooted in life, so to speak, and fame and fortune came to him as unexpected delights. I set out well-shod in his wake and felt fame and fortune were expected for me. So I snorted at the bit where he would have clopped merrily along. I blush now to think how unreasonable I must have seemed to those who had to contend with me.

I think that Americans imported from Europe the notion that the son should follow in the father's footsteps, except that abroad some training was tossed in together with allowance for the difference in ages. The son apparently was to have no choice in the matter. Here the proviso was added that he should go it alone. Here he was expected to go the old man one better because he had a boost from books.

Along with this notion goes the belief in inherited ability, which is patent nonsense. When I first went to work as sports department office boy on my father's paper, Hearst's *New York American,* an editor would holler something like "Get the cuts off the stone!" No explanation. Apparently it was assumed I was born equipped to fathom such abracadabra. I found that if I asked questions I was viewed as a congenital idiot.

Anyway I felt I had a problem of trying to meet expectations of others, real or imagined, and I know now that my father was unaware of it and couldn't have helped because he never had to contend with the same circumstances. Ironically, he was helpless to help me against my enemy that he knew so well, Demon Rum. He was depressed when I followed in his footsteps along that line, but only once did he try to take me to task.

That was when reports of my misconduct once had reached him from Washington ahead of me on one of my excursions to New York. I contacted him when

I arrived—I never went home. I knew something was up when he arranged a meeting on a street corner at 57th Street and Sixth Avenue.

I was shaky from my Capital capers. It didn't help to have him come straight from the dentist's where he'd undergone some butchery on his mouth. In foul mood, spitting blood and curses, he suggested we adjourn to a bench along Central Park South. He started hollering. All I remember is that passers-by gave us startled stares. My father usually held his steam pretty good, but he could be a caution when he did blow up.

Suddenly he broke off. He spit and shrugged. With a characteristic gesture he waved off the subject. "You," he stated with startling calm, "are going to drink until you're good and ready to quit drinking and nothing that I or anyone else says is going to stop you." He was so positive there was nothing more to say.

Now that he was moving into the shadows toward the big answer I suddenly realized that he wasn't being positive any more. He was leaving answers more to me. At least I "would not be disapproved."

We had one last row that was a real sockdolager. It started with a lengthy letter in which he explained the way he was setting up his last will in an effort to protect my sister and he sought my signature on a matter in this connection.

I took exception. Not believing in the dead hand ruling the living, I objected that he was trying to play the prophet in his final testament by attempting to make provisions so far-reaching they would affect, possibly, persons as yet unborn. I balked at his request. As it later developed I was correct, but what he didn't tell me at the time was that he already had committed himself to certain provisions that I'd questioned.

He replied in such a rage that his estate has withheld permission for direct quotation of the letter. His explosion revealed one aspect of his life with mother that never had been mentioned previously. He recalled that she had made sudden demands on him for large sums of cash which he was hard pressed to provide.

From the heat of his indignation after all these years I gathered that thoughtless spending by my mother was a major point of trouble between them. I'd known her to be fast on the pocketbook, but I didn't realize my father had been hard put at times to keep up with her checks. I grew another inch in understanding.

However, my father was throwing heavy moral obligations my way in his will and I wasn't going to wobble at this late date. I refused to fall back, mainly for my own self-discipline, although friends later told me they knew my stubborn stand would cost me materially. In fact, this standing up to my father cost me plenty in more ways than one, yet I came out winner, and so did he, although he wound up backing down. For we gained mutual respect, father for son, and through the magic medium of words which had divided the family we now shook hands. The fear was gone.

This struggle for co-existence took more emotional stamina than I'd been able to build up in the time since I'd quit drinking and started to work a change in my way of meeting life. While I was concentrating on one phase I was inclined to be testy on others.

I know now that the constant manning of inner defenses against surprise attacks by booze explained my father's bewildering changes in moods, his sudden outbursts of irritation, his brooding in depression. Both of us at times sank with weariness from the minute-by-minute fight.

For him the road of sobriety was rougher since he did not have the benefit, as I did, of a map such as that provided in the so-called Twelve Steps of Alcoholics Anonymous. I eventually reached the point where the drinking atmosphere of the republic didn't bother me.

But he was what the A.A.s called a "reformed drunk," meaning one without benefit of "The Program." For him it was a life-long fight, without surcease, and he was uneasy in the presence of strong drink. He did not like to have others boozing in his company if he could help it.

Through the A.A. program I was seeking to work a change in personality so that I could meet the world as peacefully as possible on its own terms. This can take years with some—and I was one. It's improbable the change ever will be complete, but progress suffices.

At the time I was reaching out for understanding with my father, however, I was on thin ground, as I soon found out. He'd just entered Memorial Hospital for Cancer in New York. He reported he had "flu." I, of course, suspected differently. As it developed he came out again, but a chain of events took place which jolted me and, I feared, would jolt my father at this crucial time.

I got fired.

It was ridiculous—and my fault. I argued—not once but twice—with an editor for putting my by-line over a feature story I did not write, although I covered it and reported to a rewrite man on *The Cincinnati Post*. I still was touchy about *the name*.

In Cincinnati my drinking record still haunted me despite two years' sobriety, so I went to Columbus and Chicago to look for a job. I didn't tell my father immediately because of the possible effect of this setback on him just as he had regained confidence in me. It wasn't until I was unable to get a job that I finally had to break the news.

My idea, I wrote him, was to go to a smaller city, such as Lexington, Kentucky, where I would make enough newspaper salary to live on while I concentrated on writing "outside," that is, fiction and articles.

Dear Damon:

You are right. Get a job in some town that just pays a living and keep writing fiction and articles. I am trying to sell your stories through an agent. I am advancing you $100 as a reserve fund for you. One thing I can't understand is your failure to have a typewriter. I have a portable I will send you if you like that kind. It is practically new as I never used it much.

P. S. I have no fear of your drinking again. If I did I would advise you to take the gaspipe. There would indeed be no hope for you. I don't think that ever will bother you again.

This was the only time he had offered me money since I'd left home, although I'd been down to nothing more than once. I never asked him. I accepted only because I needed to get around in a hurry to beat the shades of time.

He was trying to keep my head up. Certainly I needed encouragement. Lexington had a job but wouldn't hire me. I'd had too much experience in big cities—Cleveland, New York, Washington, Cincinnati. They didn't think I'd stay. I was getting desperate not only because I was back to bare survival.

I heard the rustling of a distant dark angel.

Dear Son:

Have been ill again with what the doctor calls intercostal rheumatism. Meaning a deep-seated pain in the chest. The agent who has your stories is working on them. He personally liked them a lot, at least "The Bomb" and one of the shorts. I will let you know when anything happens. I have a letter from Mary. Enclosed another check. You can consider these as advances and repay me when you are able, if you wish.

P. S. Have sent you a portable typewriter. Let me know when you receive it.

". . . deep-seated pain in the chest." Was he hiding the worst from me? Or didn't he know? Or was it really "intercostal rheumatism"? I had been through a siege of cancer with a member of my mother's family just two years before and knew the tricks. Now I was racing.

Talking with I.N.S. bureau men in Columbus, it dawned on me that I never was fired from I.N.S. in Washington. In 1943, I was "suspended" until such time as I was able to quit the booze. I started inquiries to see if I.N.S. would take me back. Meanwhile my father's letters got shorter and shorter like the last gasps of a dying man.

November 12, 1946

Dear Damon:

I will send you a check for $100 the first and fifteenth of the month until you get a job. You will have to make that do though I know it will be a tight fit.

I have been quite ill. Gall bladder trouble, the doctors say. I will answer your letter in more detail later.

Gall bladder trouble? Now I knew someone was kidding someone. Of course I didn't let on I knew because I didn't know if he knew. I hardly think he could have believed that. It was more likely that even in his darkest hour he was trying to help someone else by keeping the worst from me when I was struggling to right myself.

It had been two years since I'd first seen my father in the hospital for those five minutes that started us on the road to reconciliation. All that time he'd been doomed, dying by inches. Now it was possible that the doctors were telling him he had various ailments just so he wouldn't know the end was near; or perhaps he knew and was handing me a line.

I.N.S. came through with an offer to join the Chicago bureau. The bid came by wire from my father. For once, I guess, he'd got into the act in my behalf, and for once I quickly accepted without caring a whoop what anyone might say about using influence this once to get the job.

Before flatly accepting, however, I told my father I would prefer to go to New York City. I gave him a song-and-dance to cover up the fact that I knew he was worse off than he let on, or perhaps knew, and for that I reasoned I wanted to be there with him.

Just before I left the *Post* I had consulted with my father's contemporary, Carl D. Groat, the editor, about whether I should just take up and go to New York where my father could call on me if he wanted. They were the same age and I figured Groat would have a better perspective. He said no.

He pointed out that my father was waging relentless war against the dread demon stalking him. Instead of falling all of a heap he had put his hat on jack deuce and defiantly went on living and writing and making the most of what little time he had left. Groat reasoned that as long as my father was alone and *had* to keep going he would fight.

But now before I made a final move I wanted to give my father a last chance to say if he wanted me there.

Dear Damon:
Don't get the idea I am rebuffing you in your offers

to come to New York. I just think that there would not be enough for you to do around me and my way of life is peculiarly ordered and might prove dull and irksome to some. You probably would not understand my friends. Sometimes I don't myself.

Besides, and above all, I feel you should not come in here except as a personality in your own right. Socially, you are welcome at any time and for as long as you care to stay, and in fact I have kept one room empty with something like that in mind. . . .

I do not feel too well. Besides the gall bladder condition I have intercostal rheumatism which is in the walls of my chest and is murder. Take care of yourself. . . .

Right after this I received first one, then two sealed envelopes marked to be opened only upon his death, and then immediately. He instructed me to keep them where I would have access to them at any time. I carried them around with me.

Before going to Chicago I was married to a Cincinnati girl, Patricia Glazier, whom my father had heard tell about in my letters and whom he called with western politeness "Miss Pat." The last time I'd seen him he'd made discreet inquiry—"Who is Miss Pat?"—but I said I'd rather he wait and meet her personally without prior buildup from me. I didn't tell him I was married because I would have rather done so in person. I suppose I still had some hope. But the last letter to Cincinnati, a little note about my sister, carried these last words—and no hope.

151

The pain is terrific.

I worked one dark week in Chicago. I was off Saturday, December 7, 1946. Next day when I went into the office a teletype operator mentioned "a story about your father," sent the day before. It was one paragraph to the effect that he had entered Memorial Hospital for "a routine check-up." Stuff and nonsense. The I.N.S. New York bureau checked the hospital and got a report that he was the same.

Off at midnight I walked the streets in sort of a daze, wondering what was up with my father. I stood staring for some time in a shop window, without seeing, when all of a sudden the thought came to mind clear and direct: "My father is dying." I hurried to my hotel room. The phone was ringing as I came in the door. New York calling. "Your father is dying," a friend of his reported.

I.N.S. editors in New York made sure I got plane reservations and alerted bureaus in case I got stranded somewhere along the way by snowstorms. All the way in the lonely darkness of the droning plane I braced myself against the hubbub I knew would attend the passing of Damon Runyon. I kept reminding myself that no matter how bad things would be drinking wouldn't help. Would it?

8

As my plane bounced like a shuttlecock through
night mottled with snow in a race against the dark
angel, I tried mentally to rehearse for the bizarre
scenes bound to come, considering the lead character.
When the plane rose above the storm I wondered
whether I would be able to do the same in New York.

I knew I was about to shoulder some responsi-
bilities for which I had no map, except perhaps my
father's last instructions still unopened in my coat
pocket. As a reporter I knew the spectacle faced by
a famous man's family at his exit. As Damon
Runyon's son I knew I could expect almost anything
to happen.

Anyone who attains fame and fortune encounters
a peculiar type of Homo sapiens, the species Homo
hangeronus, who may be harmless, homicidal or just
plain harassing, and some of whom, more frequently
in the Broadway and sport bushes, are a hop, skip
or jump out of the paleolithic period. They can be

hard to handle, so I worried what to do if I ran into any.

There also is a strange type who dotes on letting it be known around and about, and where it will do them the most good, that they are close to the fellow in the public eye. All Homo hangeronus display this characteristic, but so do others who may even have a touch of fame and fortune themselves, which can be very confusing indeed.

I already knew how to regard the close type. On our last visit together my father and I had a set-to over my going through a leading motion picture producer to tell him in Hollywood that my sister had fallen seriously ill and needed help that I couldn't provide.

To my father's protest over going to a third party I replied, "But I understand he was very close to you."

His fingers jabbed emphatically at the keys of the typewriter he was using as a voice. He rolled the paper up so I could see what he had written. "No one is close to me. Remember that."

He cocked his head at me to make sure I was taking it in, stuck out his lower lip and clenched his teeth to show grim seriousness, then stabbed his right forefinger for added emphasis on what he'd written. He ran his finger back and forth under "Remember that."

He was preparing me for the hurly-burly into which I now was plunging. Neither he nor anyone else, however, could school me to handle the one person whose reactions worried me the most—myself. That was a job for me alone and I could not be sure what to expect.

It was two years since my elbow last burnished a bar but time was no insurance against some incident touching off a hidden spring that would cause me to flip my lid and boggle my role. Had I learned enough to stand without using a brass rail as a crutch? How could I know? I couldn't, until I'd tried.

So I landed in New York with a few hangers-on of my own, gaudy ghosts of giddy days when public toppling from tippling was no novelty with me. Running through my mind like enchanted incantations were the sayings of those who helped me help myself. A drink never solved a problem. . . . Drinking won't help. . . . Take it easy. . . . Face facts. . . .

The cold city wore a funereal gray mantle of drizzly fog matching my mood. The first problem was to find a place to park myself, for those were the days when a vacant room was as rare as hail in hell. The first setback came when the Buckingham Hotel announced that my father's three-room suite was off limits to all, including me, and no other space was available. His "friends," I gathered, had given "orders."

Standing on the street with my satchel in the dark dawn, drizzle and despair, it occurred to me that there was no confidant to whom I could turn. For all of my father's wide commerce with his fellow human beings, there was none to whom he had directed me for a helping hand at this low point.

I was too weary at that stage to do much thinking about whys and wherefores, since I had been awake from the day before when I worked my full trick in Chicago and then made a sleepless flight to New York. It just struck me as a bit ironical.

Not long before, my father and I were in the Stork Club's Cub Room, where the elite meet to sneak peeks at each other, when in came a crew haircut who looked so young I wondered how he passed the bar examination on the way. My father gave me the elbow to bring my attention to a note he'd scribbled, saying, "Bill Mauldin."

"Do you know him?" I asked. My father put on a pseudo-serious expression as he wrote, "I know everybody." He chuckled—that is, he went through the pantomime of chuckling—and motioned Mauldin over.

While he was stretching it when he said "everybody," the fact was that he knew a staggering number of people, and more who didn't stagger, besides guys and dolls. Yet here I was all alone with my satchel and sorrow. Worse, weariness worried me. I knew I should do something, such as sleep, to perk up for the ordeal ahead.

That was a dangerous time for me as an alcoholic since fatigue lowers mental and physical resistance and makes it possible for thoughts of brew to ferment freely. I never was any bargain physically, having been short-changed in the weight department, and literally shook like dice at Monte Carlo for six months after I downed my last double dram, so I had to check myself mentally as often as a hypochondriac feels his pulse.

Finally I called a member of the self-appointed corporal's guard around my father. Over the phone he squawked like a chased chicken at being awakened before noon. He said he would make reservations at a hotel two blocks from the Buckingham.

When I asked about my father I was told, "Go to sleep and we'll call you." The hotel to which he sent me gave me the upturned nose.

So I called another member of the corporal's guard. He bellowed like a steer in Chicago because I woke him up. He directed me to a Broadway hotel for guys and dolls. There I was accepted with only a few coughs behind the hand. Again, when I asked about my father I was told, "Go to bed and we'll call you if you're needed—just stay there."

Dazed by depression, a fog for my thoughts, I showered and then sat limply on the edge of the bed, trying to think what time I should get up and what next to do. My New York reception had been demoralizing and I feared flashes of foam would fetch me. My thoughts collected a little and ground 'round to another time when I was alone and faced one of the great decisions of a lifetime.

That time I had taken aboard so much bilge at bars I could barely navigate, but strangely enough for once under such a load my thinking had been lake water clear. Somehow I had steered a zigzag course, going

    teeter

       waver

      plunge

to the banks of the Ohio River where I anchored to one of the castaway big granite blocks used to line the water's edge when the paddle wheelers tied up at Cincinnati.

Sitting there I debated two choices. Either I was going to quit drinking, without hedging and for the rest of my life, or I was going to use the $43 I had left to start then and there in the waterfront saloons within sight a block away to become a wino bum who inevitably would wind up raving in jail or a city psycho ward, if I was lucky.

I had no job, no material resources or possessions, no prospects, and no one who could lift me out of that state if I didn't act to save myself. I faced the fact that life went on without me if I surrendered and withdrew. I realized that none could help me fight, no matter how much they cared, if I didn't choose myself to fight. This dawning decided me.

In the hotel room, as on the river bank, I suddenly became my own man. Out loud I cried, "Why should I take orders from those guys? My father's dying and my place is there with him!" I dressed like a smoke-eater headed for an eight-alarmer, drove a taxi driver with whips of words to beat lights, and stormed into Memorial Hospital. Within minutes I was outside the door behind which my father lay dying.

I was just getting loud with a nurse in the way when along came a wisp of a doctor who apparently had been summoned posthaste to deal with me. This was my father's physician, who looked very young and very tired. Indeed, although he evidently had no inkling, he was doomed then by his heart and himself had little life left to live. He eased me down the hall and proceeded to question me.

"I didn't know Damon had a son," he said mildly. "He never mentioned anything about family." He added that he had thought the members of the corporal's guard were the only friends close to my father. I quoted my father's remark that "no one" was "close" to him, which I had to assume as my guide. I began an explanation of the Runyon family set-up, why I had to stay in Cincinnati and Chicago, and reached for the sealed notes to show my father had expected me to see him off.

Suddenly I broke off and blew up.

"Listen," I fumed, "I don't have to give explanations to anyone. I am tired of being ordered around and questioned. My father expected me to be here and here I am and no one has the right to be telling me otherwise." I ran on heatedly in that vein until I realized that the poor man was completely taken aback and more than somewhat bewildered at my outburst.

He had been merely curious, of course, and his questions were only natural and amiably put. He meant no offense and my tirade was unwarranted. He just happened to catch me when I was primed to fire a broadside at the first person I thought might be trying to give me the run-around after my encounter with the corporal's guard. I simmered down and apologized.

"Do you want to go in?" he asked, indicating my father's room. I hadn't thought about it before, but now it occurred to me that if my father saw me there, especially since I'd just taken a new job in Chicago, he would know his luck had run out at last. The doctor said he was in a coma and wouldn't know me. "What I meant," he said, "was—well, it's rather unpleasant . . ." I insisted on going in. He shrugged and led the way.

The bright face of death was a blinding shock. I had to turn away for a moment to recover. When last

I saw my father he weighed 195 pounds. Now he was reduced to a hollow shell, almost literally, weighing perhaps 100 pounds guessing by the gaunt face. His once ruddy-brown complexion, which had suggested the weather-beaten West of Indian or cowboy, now was jaundice-yellow. Here and there, neck and hands ghastly gray told where the cancer was coming through full course.

In some cases there is little or no pain, even at the last, but in his, "The pain is terrific. . . ." He suffered longer and more intensely than he let on.

He would be sitting perhaps in the Stork Club Cub Room amid the gay and giddy when the sweat of pain would break out on his forehead. Silently, gritting his teeth, he would quickly leave the table, go into the rest room and gulp merciful medication. It got worse as time—and the creeper—went on. He refused to give up, however, even at the last.

Alone he fought fiercely.

He reeled from room to room.

His arms wildly thrashed the air.

He clenched his teeth and gripped the furniture, hard, trying to bear up.

He threw things.

Through the blinding glaze he barely saw them trying to get hold of him. He cursed soundlessly. The agony was all bottled up inside.

"Take a ride," they said, "get the air."

Anything! Anything!

Anything to try to escape the gusts of pain.

They led him out, blind from the cruel waves.

He raged wordlessly against the enormity bowing him.

But what's this? Hospital! No! Won't give up!

He balked on the steps. Through tears of torture he tried to see them.

In the hospital room he still stormed around, trying to escape the inescapable rack within, shattering even reason. He fought on.

Suddenly he cried out—his lips formed the words and the shattered lungs frantically worked a weak whisper:

"Booze! Booze! Booze!"

Why not?

"Sure. What do you want?"

The anguished figure stood swaying, the brain trying to grope through sheets of torture back through the file of misty memories. What? What? So long ago . . . Shoulders convulsing, tears streaming down the twisted face, he shook his head.

No.

Not now.

Keep fighting . . .

The agents of mercy worked swiftly.

He didn't need to fight any more.

Once, long later, he opened his eyes and dimly saw his friend, the little doctor, standing there.

He smiled. His eyes closed peacefully and he went back.

Now in the quiet room where we sat watching from two chairs at the foot of the bed the little doctor said softly, "I don't know what keeps him alive. He's gone from the waist up. . . ."

He was disintegrating before our eyes. . . .

"He was the strangest patient," the little doctor said. "It was so hard to get any information out of him about himself. Did you know he had t.b.? We found out from an X-ray. Once, not long ago, he just dropped in to see me. He obviously had something on his mind he wanted to talk over, something personal bothering him. We talked about a lot of things for an hour and then he left without ever mentioning what was bothering him, what he came to talk about. He was too shy."

He sighed and said we might as well get some rest. Tomorrow, he said. In the hospital lobby the little doctor asked what plans I had for final arrangements. I assumed they were in my father's sealed notes.

"You know your father," the little doctor said. "He may have made some strange requests that might be impossible to carry out. Don't you think you'd better open those notes now? If the requests are too fantastic we might be able to get him to change them in case he wakes up."

I debated with myself at length. The Runyons were sticklers at keeping their word and the notes were not to be opened "until death and then immediately." Finally I threw myself on the doctor's judgment. He thought they should be opened. He pointed out that the specified time was not far off anyway. The main missive said:

November 17, 1946

My dear Son:

These are your instructions for the disposal of my remains and you are not to permit anyone to dissuade you from them on any grounds.

Have Campbell's . . . take charge of body immediately on being advised of my death.

No funeral services. No display of my body. No flowers.

I desire that my body be cremated and my ashes scattered without publicity over the island of Manhattan, the place I have truly loved and that was so good to me.

I think you can get Captain Eddie Rickenbacker of Eastern Airways to get his boys to perform this service for me. If you like you may have my name added to the stone over your mother's grave in the family plot at Woodlawn.

I have often expressed these wishes about my disposition in my column and other writings so there is nothing new about them save as addressed to you personally.

In Affection,
Dad

P. S. There is a copy of these instructions in my box in the hotel office or the vault box in the Chase National Bank branch at 143 57th.

Dad

"That," I groaned, "is some order!"

"Yes," the little doctor said, "but it isn't too fantastic. I'm sure Rickenbacker will do it."

That was not what I was thinking about.

What really bothered me was that order, "without publicity." I looked at all this as a reporter, as well as a son, and I knew a colorful story when I saw one. How was I going to accomplish all that "without publicity"? Knowing my father, of course, I could understand why he wanted it that way.

He frowned on the spectacles when someone in the public eye checked out. Shy in life, he wanted no curious peeking at him in death. Without formal religion, there was nothing to say in that department. And he wanted no hordes below gaping up at the last disposal. The way he put it in another note was that he wanted "no fuss" and "get it over with quickly."

There were two other short notes. One referred to his former second wife and also made mention of my sister, who could not come from Cincinnati. The other note said:

November 22, 1946

Damon, there was another woman who came into my life, late, who was most kind to me. Her name is ———. If she likes I wish you [1] might be permitted (sic) to commune with me after I put my checks back in the rack. You will please be most kind and considerate of her. She never wanted anything from me. Not a thing. You will, of course, also be kind and considerate to all those who were my friends when I needed kindness and consideration myself.

In Affection,
Dad.

First I went to see one of the friends who had assumed charge. When I had arrived in New York he'd groaned a description of his heavy duties answering calls about my father and opening messages

[1] An obvious error. He meant "she." The late date indicated the note was written when he was in great pain.

pouring in. Why, he'd moaned, he'd torn up at least five hundred telegrams alone. I was appalled. How was the family to acknowledge them? He waved aside such fine points.

Now I explained that I had the final instructions from my father. I made the mistake of showing him the letter on arrangements, even allowing him to put a copy in his file. Also present were two more of his friends who learned the contents of the note. One of these three was an old-timer while the others were relatively late in my father's life. I figured I had to confide in someone since I was alone and might need help. Besides all pledged themselves to secrecy to avoid publicity.

On the publicity score I went to my boss of that time, Seymour Berkson, general manager of International News Service, who was one of my father's friends of long standing. He recalled how my father used to sit in his office chatting about matters which had just come to Berkson's attention or were just about to reach him in his work. This puzzled him until he finally asked my father about his powers of divination. My father explained that as a youth he had learned the typesetter's trick of reading type upside down. From where he sat in Berkson's office he could read mail and other papers on the desk although they were upside down.

Berkson at once threw his powers and those of the service into helping me carry out my father's final instructions. He was, like my father, a friend of Captain Rickenbacker, who happened to be out of town, so he would make the contact there. As for the publicity angle, we decided to go straight to the opposition and ask for co-operation as fellow gentlemen of the press in regard to one of their own. We knew we could rely on their word although technically we were "mortal enemies" in getting the news.

This integrity of the gentlemen of the press was one of the reasons my father called the fourth estate "the greatest profession." In tribute to him the press agreed to a unique arrangement for news coverage, although it was not the first time this had been done.

Berkson arranged with the opposition news services that I.N.S. would cover the funeral. Any developments would be telephoned to the Associated Press and United Press before being sent out on I.N.S. wires. This covered New York newspapers and radio since all take one or more of the wire services. The reporter on the story would be Damon Runyon, Jr.

The I.N.S. powers got me moved into the Commodore Hotel, which was a relief. My wife, a soft-spoken, gentle person, who never had been far from home, was flying from Cincinnati and I was concerned about introducing her to New York by way of the hotel for guys and dolls. When she arrived I no longer felt alone.

One of my father's old friends came up to offer us help. He was Dan McKetrick, once a sports writer on the old *New York World*, former prize fight manager, businessman, now about my father's age and sporting a long limousine and chauffeur. It was one of those ironic quirks in life that my wife and I were newlyweds, and in 1911 my father and mother had stayed on their honeymoon in Paris with the McKetricks. Dan called him Al.

I could tell how long people knew my father by the name they used. When they called him Al that dated them back at least thirty-five years, usually to Denver. Some of these, as in McKetrick's case, I had known as a small boy. A number offered help when they found I was there, but did not persist when I explained my father had left it to me to do the job more or less alone. I had a little more difficulty with some of his Broadway friends who felt they were close to him.

At the hospital I had to stop one of these from pushing around Tony Pugliese of International News Service, whom I had known for years, and who had managed to get upstairs, eluding other reporters and photographers in the lobby. Reporters who get pushed around only try harder. I got Tony to one side to deal straightforward with him.

An I.N.S. editor had sent him to try to get my father's last statement, if any, and funeral arrangements. This shows how a newspaperman keeps his word. The office didn't know that Berkson already knew. I explained to Tony I wasn't giving out the statement, that I.N.S. would get it first for the others if I did, and that I personally would square things with the editor if any question arose.

Next thing I knew the friend was trying to throw out two King Features representatives who had come to offer any help they could in behalf of King. They were Bradley Kelly and Colonel Joseph Willicombe Jr., whose late father was a right hand to

William Randolph Hearst. Kelly whispered, "We see what you are up against. Just let us know if we can help in any way."

I had to break up a scuffle at the door to my father's room when The Game Kid, a race track character, tried to go in and was blocked by the corporal's guard by self-appointment. The Game Kid was protesting loudly about how long he'd known my father and it took some diplomatic negotiations to head off a real row. Even so, The Game Kid and two of the others every now and then would fall to arguing again and I would have to shush them.

Now the gray creeper raced to full course.

My father never stirred.

A nurse wanted to run across the street to get a priest. I refused. My father made no commitment on religion and I would not assume such a purely personal right.

At 7:06 P.M., December 10, 1946, I noted a gentle breath of wind lifted apart the curtains on the window for a long moment and then dropped them gracefully back into place.

The dark angel had arrived.

The sad-faced little doctor came up to my wife and me in the hall outside the room.

"The city editor of the *Herald Tribune* is on the phone," he said wearily. "He suggests that this would be a good chance to break the silence about cancer. He wants to know if it would be all right to say that Damon died of cancer."

"Certainly," I said. "I don't object and I'm sure Dad wouldn't if it would do any good."

I hadn't thought about it before, but newspapers never reported a person dying of cancer. It was a "lingering illness." The old hat idea was that cancer was an odious disease with some stigma. Few people, if any, would admit privately, much less publicly, that they or anyone in the family suffered it. There's no telling how many thousands died because of that nonsensical attitude. Newspapers feared trouble if they reported cancer as the cause of death.

As far as I know, my father was the first person of note whose death was attributed publicly and bluntly to cancer. Even as a newspaperman I was astonished at the space given throughout the nation to his passing—many papers ran several columns of type on him—so the cause of his demise was widely circulated. Now it is common usage to mention cancer in obituaries.

The next day I was astounded when the *New York Mirror* story reported that Walter Winchell had "revealed" the essence of my father's confidential last wishes. It was a shocking breach of trust—not by Winchell, of course, but by the friend who had kept a copy of the statement which he had phoned to the columnist immediately upon my father's exit.

In fairness to Winchell, I must say that his source perhaps did not mention over the phone that the statement specified there was to be no publicity. And, I might add, I probably was foolish in the first place to let a copy get out of my hands, but then I was not familiar with that character.

I was publicly embarrassed not only in view of my pledges to my colleagues of the press, such as I.N.S., but also because the printed revelation came as a complete surprise to Captain Rickenbacker. In the *New York Daily News* columnist Ed Sullivan deplored the leak and cried, "Runyon's real friends of long standing are blazing as they learn of other fantastic things that happened just before he died."

I assume that by "fantastic things" he meant the shenanigans outside death's door, but I do not know to whom he was referring as real friends. My father freely chose his own friends, even the one who broke trust, and wrote his final scene himself. If fantastic things happened, then that was the Damon Runyon touch over all.

The job of carrying out my father's last wishes without publicity now was doubly difficult, so at Campbell's I made certain no one heard the final arrangements except the director assigned to my case, or whatever they call it in the trade. We were about to come to grips with the task when the door banged open and one of the friends flung himself in. He breathed hard over the desk at the director and demanded, "Wh-what's going on here?"

The director rose with such dignity it seemed as though sixty seconds passed before he'd unfolded fully to his lean length. Just as slowly and calmly he said, "This is a family matter. It is private. Please leave the room." After the intruder retreated in confusion the director made a little speech to the effect that Campbell's would carry out the wishes of my father and myself to the letter. He clearly saw my problem.

We began plotting.

That night The Game Kid barged into our room at the Commodore Hotel. He still was in a loud pout over the fast shunting given him by the others at the hospital. He puffed dark hints that he had some highly important secrets to impart to me. He was hurt when I showed no interest. Finally he blurted out some wild nonsense about a $1,000 overcoat belonging to my father and added that he knew things about certain parties around and about that I should be busting my clavicle to hear.

"In the first place," I said, "I don't believe even a coat of Dad's is worth $1,000 and I wouldn't want it if it was. In the second place, I don't want to hear gossip about anyone. I'm just not interested. None of it could be important to me. All I'm interested in right now is carrying out Dad's last wishes. The rest has nothing to do with me."

I do not think I got through to The Game Kid. I tried to be kind and polite, but now I was running on nerve and finally after an hour of this picking at trifles I had to ask him out bluntly. When the door closed after him my wife, who had hardly said a word, spoke up. "Now I'm beginning to understand your mother."

The phone never stopped ringing whenever we were in the room. Some old family friends called and, of course, I enjoyed cutting up old touches. But many of the calls were bizarre. Several were whispered hints along the same line spouted to us by The Game Kid, as if some back-alley conspiracy were brewing. To this day I haven't the slightest notion what it was all about, and I still don't care.

From out of the past came voices I had known somewhere, some place, some time, frequently so long ago that now they echoed in memory's chamber no more than the total strangers who called. One great lady, the gentlewoman's cultured tones now cracking with the weight of her years, addressed me familiarly as "Brother." That was my family "calling name," used to avoid confusion with my father around the house. I hadn't been called that since I was nine except for the day old friends like this woman came to bury my mother. Where do the years go?

Several dolls called. They were not dolls of Runyons, Senior or Junior, but of certain parties—all of them late parties, I believe—once known to my father. I wondered what kind of hand fate had dealt these dolls. What happened after the merry-go-round stopped? They had been silken pretties, some set in jewels, who lived high in fast company in an era when so many people were high if not fast company. How now? I was discreet enough not to ask and depressed enough not to want to know at that time.

Other calls were from known sharp operators or strangers dull enough to tip their hand. All buzzards don't fly. In most cases I never learned what they were after, although I could fairly well guess the pitch, for I politely ducked any proposed contacts. These ghouls really bowed my spirits. I tired quickly of being a target at such a time. Finally one caller gave me ten minutes of patter building himself up as close to my father. I patiently uh-huh'd him, waiting for the twister. He wanted my father's shoes since they were too small to fit me.

I pointed out that my father had departed less than twenty-four hours previously, that the will hadn't been read, and I had no powers except to dispose of his bodily remains. I hung up and then blew up. After that I refused all calls unless they were from I.N.S. or Cincinnati, my wife's home.

No notice was placed in newspapers. If you knew Damon Runyon you would know where he most likely would be "reposing," as they say in the trade.

The room was open only from 5 P.M., December 11 to midnight.

No funeral services—no display—no flowers. That's the way it was—well, we did hedge a trifle on the flowers.

The room chosen looked more like the living room of a swank hotel suite.

Standing at one end was a big dark brown box on a stand. The lid was closed. This touch, together with the absence of the usual formidable array of overpowering flowers, dispelled the funereal air. It was more like a dry farewell party for a departing friend. The only flowers were a small bunch of roses someone talked us into putting on top of the casket with the card "The Family."

Those who streamed in included greats and small of Broadway, sports, Hollywood, the fourth estate and assorted worlds, including guys and dolls, and silent underworld characters who walked quickly to the closed casket where they stood for a moment and then wheeled and left as wordlessly as they came while plainclothesmen there for the same purpose looked the other way.

At precisely midnight the door was closed to visitors until 1 A.M. when my wife and I arrived. What happened in the interim? Why, the "mystery woman" slipped in, of course, according to formula.

Early the morning of December 12, 1946, a slick black limousine purred west on 72nd Street and parked at the corner of Broadway by a five-and-ten-cent store. The parties inside the car sat waiting for a certain party to come along. They plotted to take him for a last ride.

Gangster goings-on?

No—Damon Runyon's funeral.

In the car were my wife and I, the director and a chauffeur. All we lacked was the deceased. Where was he? We had plotted to get him out of the funeral establishment without being trailed by reporters and photographers or anyone else.

Originally I had agreed that a few mourners would go along, although I feared others would be hurt when they heard about it. My father seemed to have left such details up to me and I gave in under pressure on that score.

Then I was approached by one of the three friends of my father's who had seen the last request on arrangements and had sworn not to reveal them. (Of course, I exclude the little doctor and Berkson from all this because I never doubted that I could confide in them as professional men.)

This man, not the one who called Winchell, said

174

that he had been talking with a prominent Roman Catholic layman and they had decided that it would be nicer, as he put it, if I had my father buried beside my mother in Woodlawn Cemetery rather than have him cremated as he requested.

I was flabbergasted. I was double whammed. Not only was the confidential information bandied in conversation, but the poor fellow could not see what was wrong with discussing the matter with a friend of my father's, although I pointed out that if friends all knew about it the statement would be public knowledge.

Furthermore I was amazed that the two men would vote to veto a friend's last plea as to his disposition. The point behind it, I knew, was a religious objection to cremation. But my father was not of that religion, nor of any formal faith. And if he was buried I would have to ignore the rest of his dying request. To this day, I confess, I am unable to fathom such thinking.

I made an effort to be polite as possible under the circumstances in rejecting this strange proposal, but inwardly I was so steamed up at this second breach of confidence that I determined that the family alone was going to carry on after the curtain at Campbell's. In fact I made a news statement to the effect that my father had belonged to the public in life; now he was to belong to his family.

So the funeral was reduced to the family, meaning my wife and me. The plan was to divide forces and meet at an appointed hour at 72nd Street and Broadway. The idea was that if one car was followed the driver would just roam around until the trail was lost. If the other car didn't show up at the rendez-vous, the rest of the party was to proceed to the crematory in Hartsdale, New York. I didn't see how Campbell's would get the body out without being noticed.

Minutes passed and we speculated whether the other driver was touring town with my father. I got out in the gloomy drizzle to case the corner. Lo, there was the other car, my father in back, parked on Broadway around the corner. It looked like a toney town car, enclosed in back, so no one along the way suspected our mission.

At the last I gave way to a feeling that there should be a touch of sentimental symbolism to this unorthodox affair. The two cars went north on the Big Street, past the homes we had known, then detoured a little to pass Woodlawn where my mother was buried alone on a high hill in a section where, as she said in selecting it, "I will meet a lot of interesting people if it turns out to be true that they walk around at night in cemeteries."

My father's expressed hope on this score was that he would be in a happy state if he "woke up dead" and found himself at a big poker game with his departed pals—"TAD" Dorgan, Sid Mercer, Matty Matthewson, Hype Igoe, and all the rest. He hoped, my father said, that they would have held a seat open for him.

December 18, 1946, my wife and I went secretly to Campbell's where I was handed a bulky package, wrapped in brown paper tied with thick twine, carefully prepared to conceal the shape. Inside was a heavy bronze urn containing the ashes of Damon Runyon. At Eastern Airlines headquarters in Rockefeller Center we met Captain Rickenbacker.

From LaGuardia Airport we went up in a big twin-engine transport with chief pilot John F. Gill at the controls along with co-pilot Captain Eddie Barber, both of whom had known my father. Rickenbacker, my wife and I, with the urn on my lap, sat in bucket seats in the rear of the plane.

The ship droned north and banked over Woodlawn. Then it bore through the dreary day down the Hudson River and turned at 3,000 feet over the Statue of Liberty. Captain Rickenbacker took the urn and went forward to the co-pilot's seat on the right of the cockpit. I stood right behind, bent over in the little companionway.

The plane steadied north over Broadway. Captain Rickenbacker tied the wrapping twine from his twist to the heavy bronze container as insurance against a slip. At Times Square I nodded and Captain Rickenbacker tipped the urn out the cockpit window.

Nothing was said aloud.

Walter Winchell already had launched a Damon Runyon Memorial Cancer Fund. The original idea was to finance one room in his memory at Memorial Hospital for newspapermen suffering cancer and lack of money. To even Winchell's surprise, the fund snowballed across the nation, until the $8,000,000 mark was passed by 1954. The fund was turned to finance research and researchers in the search for an answer to cancer.

My part was in allowing the press to pinpoint the cause of my father's death and thereby break the silence and the idea of stigma about cancer. At the time I was thinking specifically in terms of promotion of freedom of the press and the right of people to know. Advancement of a crusade against cancer was secondary in mind, since that would follow freedom's footsteps. The Runyon Memorial Fund came as a surprise to me since the family was not consulted.

At first, I confess, my reaction was only human. I was more than somewhat miffed by the oversight. I believe it was an oversight of the moment. The fund sprang out of emotion. Oversights and overslights were inevitable. I did not question the cause, of course, but I was not sure I cared for the use of the name. Although I had nothing to say about it I had to contend with the inevitable cranks, crackpots and curious. After a time this gets mighty annoying. The fund also could be depressing to a Runyon.

At first I attended some of the ceremonies involving the fund, such as payment of the first check at a do in the Stork Club, but I found that each of these affairs was for me like another funeral.

Once the fund got going I naturally could not protest, even if I'd a mind to, for that would have made me look bad. Since then, of course, I realized that great good overwhelms the private considerations of one family. I am merely reporting candidly some backstage scenes and thoughts. If it never did anything else the fund accomplished a wonderful gain by smashing another senseless stigma and getting the foe into the open so it can be fought, and I am all for that. Certainly it is a memorial that beats stone.

Some figure fanatic figured that Damon Runyon wrote 60,000,000 words in his time for the information or entertainment, or both, of the public. I have not counted to check, but the estimate sounded low and didn't include the millions of words written for the wastebasket, which all writers must feed in the years required to mold their talent for actual sales.

As a short story writer he commanded the highest price of his time, one dollar for each word. He also may have been the highest salaried reporter. On the I.N.S. payroll at his death he was carried with the rank of reporter at $35,000 a year. This was aside from his salary on other payrolls such as those of King Features Syndicate and Hearst Newspapers. I have no inkling of the total newspapers paid him. He pulled $2,000 a week in Hollywood.

Although he spent a lot, loving the first class life as he did, he left a relatively sizeable estate, all things considered. In his letters to me he moaned as if he were a candidate for potter's field when in fact he was what the majority of people, including myself, would call rich. Deep within all of us remain the little children of yesteryear. When the man Runyon cried "Broke! Broke!" he was feeling the panic of the lonely little barefoot boy of Manhattan, Kansas, Pueblo, and other parts of the West.

Of course at the last he was struck with the tremendous burden of my sister's illness which in the wake of his own gave cause for financial alarm, but not as much as he implied.

He still had $25,000 cash in the bank. He left a stack of literary property, the actual stories, which can be sold or leased for such projects as motion pictures and plays. This way his estate pulls an income as long as anyone wants to read Runyon. The Broadway musical, *Guys and Dolls,* was based on one of my father's short story plots. While he did not write the actual show it must pay a percentage to the estate. In fact, I had to pay the estate to use my father's letters to me.

For the record, I do not share any proceeds from the estate but live by labor and loans like millions who can get a library card without having the librarian squeal, "Oooo, are you *really* the son of . . ." Half the income of my father's estate was left to care for my sister; the other half went by separation agreement to his second wife who had divorced him and married a young man. He also gave her everything else, from Florida house to books, except his personal jewelry and clothes.

Material possessions never possessed him. Once he was looking through his jewelry, a hobby with him, when he suddenly held up a costly watch and announced, "I'd sell that, right now, for a price." No rush of bidders pressed him, as I was the only other person in the room. This was one of my father's object lessons, with props, so I looked alert for the point to come with Barrymorean flourish. "Never," he added solemnly, "get so attached to material things that you can't bear to part with them." He left the jewelry and whatever else remained of his personal possessions to the auction block. There wasn't much. The jewelry he'd carried so suavely—

gold cigarette case with signature in diamonds, big gem rings, trick watches, fancy lighters forever failing—out of their setting looked sadly like Broadway dross.

Sentimental gewgaws, like his World War I correspondent's identification bracelet, he left with a note for my sister and me in a safe deposit box. They were seized by the estate and I had to buy them for $110. I wouldn't have purchased them if the sentiment hadn't been there for my sister. The sentiment was a little late. About thirty-two years too late. Or was it longer than that? Wasn't it as late as the days and nights when a barefoot little boy roamed dusty streets of Pueblo, Colorado, lonely and frightened too?

THE END

ABOUT THE AUTHOR

BORN IN New York City on June 17, 1918, Damon
Runyon, Jr. was educated in public and private schools
there, as well as in Bronxville and Washington; also at
Riverside Military Academy, Gainesville, Georgia. Though
nearly buried in a flurry of copy paper on his bewildering
childhood visit to a city newsroom, with his father, he
didn't really join the fourth estate till much later when he
became a sports office boy on the old *New York American.*
After leaving school he took a job with United Press in
Cleveland, becoming night bureau manager. In 1938 he
went to International News Service, New York, transfer-
ring a month later to its Washington bureau. He also worked
briefly for the *Washington Times-Herald* and Transradio
Press Service. In 1944 he moved on to Cincinnati's Radio
Station WSAI as news editor, continuing in that city with
the *Cincinnati Post* until 1946. After another brief stint with
I.N.S. in New York, he worked for the *New York Journal-
American* for four years. At present he is a news-feature
writer on *The Miami Daily News* in Miami, Florida, where
he lives with his wife, Patricia, and two children, D'Ann
and Damon III. His hobbies are photography, jazz records
and hi-fi.